FOREST MANAGEMENT IN TRIBAL AREAS

About the Editors

A member of the Indian Administrative Service for 33 years, **Pyarimohan Mohapatra** had served long years in the tribal areas of the State and developed a deep commitment towards the cause of the tribals. A post-graduate from Allahabad University, Mohapatra also did a spell at London School of Economics producing a paper on Investment and Pricing Policy in the Public Sector with special reference to Steel Industry. Currently Director General of Training, Mohapatra has held several key positions in Government, the last being Development Commissioner-cum-Additional Chief Secretary.

Profullo Chandro Mohapatro Ph.D. has to his credit long years of research into the burning economic issues of the tribal areas. A prolific writer of research based articles which have been published in most Academic Journals in India, Dr. Mohapatro presented a paper on the Problems of Weaker Classes in India at a seminar on Public Policy and Income Distribution in the University of Sussex, UK. Currently he is engaged in teaching, post-doctoral research as well as the Director of COATS.

FOREST MANAGEMENT IN TRIBAL AREAS

Forest Policy and Peoples Participation

(Proceedings of the Seminar, Forest Policy and Tribal Development during 15-16 February 1994 at Koraput)

Edited by

P.M. MOHAPATRA
Chairman
Council of Analytical Tribal Studies
D.N.K. Road, Koraput-764020

DR. P.C. MOHAPATRO
Director
Council of Analytical Tribal Studies
Koraput

CONCEPT PUBLISHING COMPANY, NEW DELHI-110059

ISBN 81-7022-671-6

First Published 1997

Published and Printed by
Ashok Kumar Mittal
Concept Publishing Company
A/15-16, Commercial Block, Mohan Garden
NEW DELHI-110059 (India)

Phones : 5504042, 5554042
Fax : 091-11-5558898

The view, if any, expressed in any articles of this book, is of the author and not of the Editors or the Council. The Editors/Council are in no way responsible for the same.

FOREWORD

The forest economy of India as well as of the state of Orissa has steadily deteriorated during the last half century, and along with it the condition of the people, mainly the tribal people, living in and around the forests and depending on the forests for their living. Official figures show that the physical output of timber, bamboo and fuelwood—the main products from the forests—steadily increased till the middle of the seventies after which it has steadily declined. In Orissa, the data presented in the paper by Drs. Sahu and Das show that during the three decades from 1960 to 1990 the annual physical output of the three main products from the forests of Orissa—timber, fuelwood and bamboo—declined by 40 to 60 per cent. Even the minor forest products show significant decline except for *Kendu* leaf, *Sal* seeds, vegetable and oil seeds, and drugs.

If the total forest area remains unchanged, the proper execution of working plans—a century old device in forest management—would ensure a steady output of the different forest products, unless there is a deliberate attempt to change the product mix in the forests. The steadily increasing output of the main forest products till about the middle of the seventies was due to over-exploitation of the forests. Obviously, this could not have gone on indefinitely. The inevitable decline started thereafter, and is continuing.

The decline cannot be attributed to the loss of forest area through legal processes for irrigation, roads, railways, industry, mines and other purposes. This accounted for hardly two lakh hectares. Bulk of this was lost before 1960; hardly twenty-six thousand hectares were lost between 1970 and 1990. During the 15 years, 1975-1991, while the recorded forest area declined by a million hectares, the difference between the recorded forest area and the area with at least ten per cent crest density was two million hectares, most of which had no or very little worthwhile forest cover. The loss is due to over-exploitation, legally and illegally. In view of this, it is inconceivable that the declining trend in major forest products can be checked and reversed in the near future.

While the forest area to be preserved for steady exploitation has been steadily and sharply declining, it is amazing that the cost of protecting this forest area and exploiting it legally has increased many times, in real terms. In 1965 the per hectare total expenditure of the Forest Department was only about Rs. 2.30. By 1990-91, this average cost per recorded forest area had risen to Rs. 65.87. Since the bulk of this cost is salary and allowances of staff, the per hectare cost of 1965 can be expressed in 1990-91 prices by using an appropriate consumer price index. The prices had risen 5.51 times during this period; therefore, the average cost in 1965 at 1990-91 prices can be put at Rs. 12.51. This means that the per hectare cost of preserving the forest of the State, in real terms, had risen 5.27 times during these 25 years. If we compare the cost per hectare of recorded area in 1965 with the cost per hectare of area with at least ten per cent crest cover in 1990-91, the cost appears to have gone up 6.38 times. It means that while the total forest area to be protected as well as the total annual produce from the forest is steadily and sharply declining, the cost to the department of preserving this declining asset is rising phenomenally. It is not surprising that while in 1965 the expenses formed 38 per cent of the gross receipts, by 1990-91 it was a little less than half. This is the sorry picture of the oldest and one of the largest public enterprises in the country. While the State is losing through declining production and rising share of expenditure in the gross receipts, the only people who appear to gain are the employees of the forest department.

Besides the State, the people who have been losing in the process are the people who live in the vicinity of or within the forest. These people are of broadly two types. One, the residents of settled agricultural villages near the forest who depend upon the forest for domestic requirements of timber, fuelwood, grass and grazing facility for cattle, and collection of minor forest produce. The second are the people in small villages and habitats within or in the vicinity of the forest who have little land fit for cultivation and who depend on the forest in a variety of ways for their living. Besides free supply of fuelwood and timber for household use, these people have traditionally depended on the forest in three other ways. They used to practise shifting cultivation, with a twelve to fifteen years cycle, on the vast forest lands. They collected fruits and roots from the forest for their food. And, they used to earn wages by working as cutters and transporters of timber from inside the forest.

While the declining forest area and cover on the one hand and the growing population on the other have reduced the availability of the necessary resources to the people of the first type, the restrictions on their traditional rights from time to time by the forest department have made the more aggressive or the needy and desperate ones to break the law and steal, thereby contributing to the destruction of forest resources.

The second type of people are mainly tribals. The increase in their population on the one hand and the declining forest area on the other, has resulted in the shifting cultivation cycle coming down from more than a decade to only a few years. The result is permanent patches with little vegetation, loss of timber, increased soil erosion and poorer yields for the shifting cultivators. The fruits and roots are now much less, and so is the wage work in the forest as indicated by the declining production. In order to survive, these people systematically steal bamboo and timber and fuelwood from the forest.

The recognition of these problems finally led to the New Forest Policy Resolution of the Government of India in 1988. A number of papers in this volume refer to this policy statement and its implications. There is a recognition of the traditional rights on forest produce of both the tribals and others living near the forest. There is a willingness to transfer rights on the village forest land to the Panchayat for community use. There is emphasis on tree planting on one's own and public lands by villagers for their individual and communal use. On degraded forest lands there is a policy of permitting tree planting by individuals with right to harvest the tree by sharing revenue with the forest department that owns the land. And, of course, there is the policy of forming village level committees for protection of the forest nearby.

While many of these are an improvement on the earlier restrictive and negative approach with regard to the rights of the local population, the sense of ownership and revenue right of the State appear still very strong. A tribal can plant a tree on the forest department's land and nurture it. What he gets is a lease right on that tree, but not on the land on which he may plant many such trees if he chooses. And, when the time for harvest comes, the planter must share a part of the gross revenue with the forest department, since the State is the owner of the land. In Orissa this rent is fifty per cent of the value of the tree! During the last half century, State Government after State Government have passed laws severely restricting such rack renting in agricultural land, finally abolishing, in many States, tenancy by transferring ownership to the tenants. And, now, in 1988, the State Government is legalising such rack renting on forest tree leases to tribal and non-tribal villagers!

There is a strange reluctance to recognise that the tribals living within or near the forests have no chance of acquiring enough land fit for agriculture or being absorbed in alternative employment opportunities.

Under such circumstances, to ask them to form committees to protect the forest in return for their right to collect fuelwood and timber and fruits and roots for their domestic use is a cruel joke. There is a complete reluctance to lease out the forest lands with no worthwhile cover today to the tribal households on nominal rent for sylviculture, which is the only possible alternative open to them, if the government wills.

The data for Orissa show that in 1990-91 there were a million hectares of recorded forest land on which there was little or no worthwhile cover—the satellite picture showed they had less than ten per cent crest cover. Another two million hectares of forest land had ten to forty per cent crest cover. There are about 1.4 million households of tribals in the State out of whom, I guess, about a million or less would be living in and around forests. It means, there is at least one hectare and at most three hectares per such tribal household which the forest department can lease out to the tribal on usufructuary basis for sylviculture. This, of course, is only an arithmetic calculation to highlight the feasibility of the proposition. A systematic effort in this direction cannot only provide a very reasonable economic basis for living to these people, but simultaneously help expand and develop forests in the State as no other policy is likely to do in the foreseeable future. It is better to make tribals small foresters, rather than go on spending more and more to protect less and less of forest land in the State. The Government of India appears to be willing and anxious to lease out land for forestry to large private companies. Then, where is the objection to leasing land out to tribal households to do sylviculture?

Pune
July 21, 1995

NILAKANTHA RATH

PREFACE

The present book is the edited volume of sixteen papers. One of the papers included in this volume is on, "An Approach to Tribal Development." This paper was presented by Dr. Neelakantha Rath, Former Director of Gokhale Institute of Politics & Economics, and at present associated with the Indian School of Political Economy, Pune; in a one day seminar organised by COATS on 17th January 1994.

The last two papers, i.e., one on 'Soil Erosion and Deforestation in Koraput District' and the other on Medicinal Plants used by tribals of Koraput district were collected from the subject experts to make this volume more useful.

As many as Sixteen papers in this book were presented in a Seminar on "Forest Policy and Tribal Development," organised by COATS on 15th and 16th February 1994 in collaboration with Sabari Cultural Society, Bhubaneswar, District Environmental Society, Koraput and two leading cultural centres of this area i.e., Sri Sri Jagannath Mandir Parichalana Sanstha, and Tribal Museum both located at Koraput.

The main objective of the seminar was to discuss various facets of forest policy in relation to tribal development and recommend a set of measures which may help the government for formulation of suitable policy measures with regard to tribal development.

The seminar was a notable one, in the sense that administrators and forest officials, professors and scholars working on the subject, tribal representatives of voluntary organisations and general public were brought together on a single platform to deliberate on the subject and to make some concrete recommendations on important issues.

In the plenary session of the seminar fourteen important resolutions were adopted unanimously by the participants. These have been sent to appropriate authorities for their consideration.

In the inaugural address, Shri B.C. Patnaik, Principal Secretary to Government of Orissa, Forest & Environment Department highlighted the policies enunciated by the State for tribal welfare relating to important issues like regularisation of encroachment on forest land, elimination of intermediaries and raising plantation of minor forest produce. He also pointed out how Government of Orissa is trying to implement the scheme of Joint Forest Management to make the Forest Department and villagers of adjacent villages of forest as equal partner in the task of regeneration and restoration of degraded forests and protection of reserved and protected forests from fire, illicit felling, theft and encroachment.

Prof. L.K. Mahapatra, a doyen of anthropology in the State and former Vice-Chancellor of Utkal and Sambalpur Universities in his keynote address "Parameters of Forest Policy for Tribal Development" argued that the forests in Koraput district managed by the tribal people were in much better condition of growth than the forests managed by Forest Department under the British Government. He hailed the decision of the Chief Minister of Orissa to grant property rights in cultivated land—as terrace, swiddens or uplands upto 30° slope and pleaded for the extension of the same right to the tribals of other parts of the State.

Prof. B.N. Das and Dr. N.C. Sahu in their paper entitled, "Forest Policy of Orissa: A Third Visit," have laid emphasis on the significant changes which have taken place in the approach towards the economic-ecologic system at global, national and regional levels. While scanning through the utilisation of forest wealth during the last four decades the authors have expressed their concern on the extent of officially denuded area of forests for various development purposes, the clandestine removal of forest produce from the ban areas and the fall in the output of most of the forest produces.

Sri Nimai Bhai, a founder member of one of the oldest voluntary agencies in the region named Banabharati, in his paper on "Towards a New Forest Policy" has condemned the new forest policy on the ground that it has overlooked the interest of poor forest dwellers. He has emphasised that only reserve forests which are now under actual tree cover may be owned by the government and for all other varieties of land in the forest, land record may be assigned to the forest dwellers taking into account individual and community needs.

Sri Jagannath Shroff in his paper on "Forest Policy and Tribal Development" has called for development of social and mixed forestry and emphasised the direct participation of the people in the implementation of these projects.

Dr. P.C. Mohapatra in his paper on "Forest Policy and Tribal Deprivation" has made a review of various forest policies enunciated from time to time and emphasised how they have always tried to restrict the rights and privileges of tribals on forest resources. While the author has commended the people oriented welfare approach of New Forest

Policy of 1988, he also has pointed out a number of deficiencies in the New Policy to inculcate the spirit of participation of the tribals in the protection and development of forest.

Dr. C.R. Mohapatra in his paper on "Podu—An Ecological Hazard" expresses his concern over the environmental degradation due to 'Podu cultivation' and calls for ensuring the sustained interest of tribals in the protection of forests.

Dr. K. Nana Buchi in his paper on, "Shifting Cultivation and Its Impact on Forest Eco-System," has suggested to create awareness in the minds of the tribals about the hazard of this practice, large scale plantation of fruit bearing trees, ensuring employment opportunities to the resettled tribals and motivate the tribals to take up settled cultivation to wean them away from this evil practice.

Sri B.N. Thakur, in his paper on 'Impact of shifting cultivation on Forest Eco-System', highlighted on the various measures undertaken by the State Government for checking the evil methods of shifting cultivation and suggested to take up a multi-directional approach to achieve the goal of controlling shifting cultivation.

Dr. Jagabandhu Samal in his paper on "Role of Forest in a Poor Resource Based Tribal Economy—A Micro Analysis," has made an indepth village study in a tribal dominated region. The author has reached the conclusion that shifting cultivation is no more rewarding and has suggested allotment of 3 to 5 acres of land per family under usufructuary heritable lease for cultivation of bamboo which is abundantly available in the region to improve the socio-economic conditions of tribals of the area.

Sri Achyut Das, in his paper on 'Joint Forest Management in Tribal Areas: Conflicts and Resolutions', noted the variability of management of forest at the village/panchayat level and status of Joint Forest Management in different States. He has raised various possible conflicts which arise out of the existing framework in the forest management and has suggested for a shift in the emphasis in the priorities attached at present to various needs.

Dr. S.P. Gantayat, in his paper, "A Look at Tribals and Forest" has discussed the symbiotic relationship between forest and tribals. The author has advocated for massive afforestation and reforestation programme by careful selection of plant species taking into consideration the local conditions and associating the local people in the programme.

Dr. B.B. Mishra, in his paper on "Tribal Women and Forest Economy," has highlighted the fact that compared to tribal males, tribal women shoulder greater responsibility of their households. The author has pointed out the difficulties faced by tribal women due to deforestation and has suggested few measures to improve the protection and regeneration of forests.

Dr. Nilakantha Rath, in his paper, "A Note on Approach to Tribal Development", has suggested suitable approaches to tribal area development taking into account the varied ecological conditions in tribal villages of Koraput region.

Sri D.K. Pattanaik in his paper on "Soil Erosion and Deforestation in Koraput District", has viewed the causes of deforestation and soil erosion in Koraput region as a hydra headed issue and called for a number of measures for scientific management of land with soil conservation measures.

Dr. M.K. Mishra, and Sri S.S. Das in their paper on, "Medicinal Plants used by the Tribals of Koraput District, Orissa", have reviewed the medicinal uses of 89 plants of Koraput district and has suggested for protection of these plants for the future use of tribals.

A number of vital issues concerning the framing of a New Forest Policy suiting to the needs of the economy has been discussed at length by the authors. The book will be of immense help to the scholars, administrators and policy-makers on the subject.

The Council is grateful to Dr. Neelakantha Rath, for giving a Foreword to its first publication. The Council is equally grateful to all the participants, authors, organisers particularly to the Secretary of Sri Sri Jagannath Mandir Parichalana Sanstha who took great care to make detailed arrangement for the seminars.

We also take the opportunity to convey our sincere thanks to Concept Publishing Company, New Delhi, who readily accepted the responsibility for publication of this volume and released it in time.

Koraput

P.M. MOHAPATRA
and
P.C. MOHAPATRO

CONTENTS

LIST OF TABLES

LIST OF CONTRIBUTORS

Nimai Bhai, Bana Bharati, Koraput, Orissa-764020.

K. Nana Buchi, Reader in Economics, Vikram Dev College, Jeypore (Koraput).

B.N. Das, Former Professor of Economics, Berhampur University, Bhanja Bihar, Berhampur-760007, Orissa.

Achyut Das, Director, Agragamee, Kashipur (Orissa) and Former Member, State Planning Board, Government of Orissa.

S.P. Gantayat, Reader in Botany, D.A.V. College, Koraput.

Malaya Kumar Misra and **Sudhansu S. Dash**, Ecology & Floristics Laboratory, Department of Botany, Berhampur University, Berhampur-760007 (Orissa).

B.B. Mishra, Head P.G. Department of Education, D.A.V. College, Koraput.

C.R. Mohapatra, Former Chairman, State Pollution Control Board, Bhubaneswar-751007.

L.K. Mohapatra, Former Professor of Anthropology & Vice-Chancellor of Utkal & Sambalpur Universities, Orissa.

P.C. Mohapatro, Director, Council of Analytical Tribal Studies, Koraput.

P.M. Mohapatra, Chairman, Council of Analytical Tribal Studies, Koraput.

B.C. Patnaik, Former Principal Secretary to Government of Orissa, Forests and Environment Department, Bhubaneswar.

Deepak Kumar Pattanaik, Lecturer in Botany, D.A.V. College, Koraput.

Nilakantha Rath, Former Director of Gokhale Institute of Politics & Economics, Pune-4

N.C. Sahu, Head of the Post-Graduate Department of Economics, Berhampur University, Bhanja Bihar, Berhampur-760007, Orissa.

Jagabandhu Samal, Reader in Economic, D.A.V. College, Koraput.

Jagannath Shroff, O.A.S. (Retd.), Treasurer, Sri Sri Jagannath Mandir Parichalana Sanstha, Koraput.

B.N. Thakur, Asst. Conservator of Forests, Koraput.

1

INAUGURAL ADDRESS

— *B.C. Patnaik, I.A.S.* *

I deem it a privilege to attend the Seminar on "Forest Policy and Tribal Development" today. The subject is as appropriate as topical.

The principal objectives of National Forest Policy is to ensure environmental stability and maintenance of ecological balances. This objective is sought to be achieved by increasing forest cover substantially in the country through massive afforestation and social forestry programmes; meeting the requirements of fuel wood, fodder and minor produce; increasing the productivity of forests to meet growing needs of the people and checking soil erosion and denudation in catchment areas. The National Forest Policy emphasised the need for massive peoples' involvement for achieving these objectives.

The Policy envisages that atleast one-third of the total land area is under forest or tree cover. The National Forest Policy, 1988 has ushered in a change in our traditional attitude to forest. Earlier forests were considered as a "source of revenue." Now it is viewed as a "capital asset" for conservation of bio-diversity and meeting the requirement of fuel wood, fodder, minor forest produce etc. of the people. The forests are not meant for commercial exploitation. The emphasis is on conservation, besides satisfying minimum needs of the rural community.

Another important thrust of the Forest Policy is involvement of village community in the forest protection and natural regeneration of forests. Towards this end Government of India issued guidelines in June 1990 on Joint Forest Management (J.F.M.), which is another important fallout of New Forest Policy. In terms of Joint Forest Management Policy local people protect forest; assist in regeneration of Degraded forests.

* Principal Secretary to Government of Orissa, Forest & Environment Department Bhubaneswar.

The State Government have been implementing the scheme of Joint Forest Management since 1st August 1988. Government issued a Resolution in August 1988 introducing the scheme of Joint Forest Management for protection of reserved forest adjoining their villages.

The scope of the scheme was further enlarged in 1990 to include protected forests. In terms of the scheme villagers were made responsible for fire protection, prevention of illicit felling, theft of forest produce, encroachment of reserved and protected forest areas. They were entitled to obtain their bonafide requirement of small timber, firewood for household consumption.

As this scheme did not have desired effect Government issued another Resolution on 3rd July 1993. The new scheme of Joint Forest Management envisage that Forest Department and villagers of the adjacent villages will be the equal partners in the task of regeneration and restoration of degraded forests.

This scheme operates in the degraded forest land both reserve and protected forest with potential for regeneration. This scheme envisages constitution of Vana Samrakshana Samiti. The Vana Samrakshana Samiti shall include two adults from every household living in the village including those who enjoy rights, concessions or privileges over the forest area. One member of each household should be a woman. Each V.S.S. is required to constitute Executive Committee with Naib Sarpanch as Chairman. The duties of the Committee include protection of the forest against grazing, fire, illicit felling, theft of forest produce and encroachment on forest land.

The main thrust of Joint Management Plan drawn up by Government relates to preparation of Joint Forest Management Plan. ACF or Range Officer concerned will prepare a Joint Forest Management Plan by carrying out microplanning exercise. Soil and water conservation measures form an integral part of the Joint Forest Management Plan. The Plan would be dove-tailed with the existing working plans. The plan will take care of the fuel, fodder, small timber requirement of people. The tree cropping pattern should provide for suitable tree mix to meet the requirement of fodder, fuel timber and other forest produce.

Successful implementation of this Joint Forest Management Scheme will go a long way in safeguarding the interests of the tribals.

Coming to the question of tribal forest interface the national forest policy has recognised the symbiotic relationship between tribal people and forest. It has also recognised the imperative need to associate the tribal people closely in the protection, regeneration and development of forest besides providing gainful employment to people living in and around the forest.

Forest Policy lays down that the rights and concessions enjoyed by tribals should be fully protected. Their domestic requirement of fuel wood, fodder, minor forest produce and construction timber should be the first charge on forest produce.

Tribal forest interface relate to such items as regularisation of encroachment on forest land and other land related problems; dispute regarding pattas/leases/grants involving forest land; elimination of intermediaries; and payment of fair wages to labourers; conversion of forest land to revenue land and payment of compensation for loss of lives and property due to degradation by wild animals and sharing of minor forest produce.

As regards regularisation of encroachment on forest land it is the policy of Government to regularise pre-1980 encroachments when decision has been taken before 25th October 1980, i.e., enactment of Forest Conservation Act to regularise eligible category of encroachment. To discourage further encroachment it is the policy of Government not to regularise post-1980 encroachments. I would like to have the benefits of discussion of this seminar regarding issues connected with settlement of pre-1980 encroachments.

Similarly, issues relating to dispute regarding patta, leases may be highlighted so that appropriate remedial action can be taken at the Government level.

Coming to the question of elimination of intermediaries, Orissa is one of the pioneer States which nationalised Kendu leaf trade way back in the year. With the nationalisation of bamboo trade in the year 1988 forest contractors have been eliminated. OFDC has been appointed as an agent of the State Government to operate bamboo trade. It has been the policy of Government and the Corporation to ensure that minimum wages are paid to bamboo cutters and tribals. In Orissa, Government has taken another step to protect and preserve forests which would safeguard the interests of tribals. Felling has been banned throughout the State from November 1993 for one year. State Government thus have eliminated the contractors from the forest.

Coming to the question of minor forest produce Government has notified 25 minor forest produces. Leases are granted only to cooperatives and corporate besides like TDCC, OFDC and Utkal Forest Produce. In this connection one issue come to my mind. It is to increase the area under plants producing minor forest produce. To increase the area under plants producing minor forest produce from which tribals eke out a living Centrally Sponsored Scheme for raising plantation of minor forest produce including medicinal plants is in operation. This scheme is in operation in the districts of Mayurbhanj, Dhenkanal, Sundargarh, Sambalpur, Keonjhar, Ganjam, Kalahandi and Koraput. During this year the target was 100 hectares in Koraput district against the total State target of 1450 hectares. The species include Harida, Bahada, Amla, Arrarut, Karanja, Char, Neem, Sabai, Bamboo, Cane, Genduli, Khair, Hill broom, Tamarind, Arjun, Red Sandal, Asana, Kanchan, Jackfruit, Sumul, Jamun, Mango etc. This scheme primarily benefit tribals.

Micro Plans for Integrated Waste Land Development Project in Laxmipur Block and Lamptaput Block in Koraput District are in operation. These micro plans for integrated waste land development project envisage restoration of waste land and meeting essential needs of fuel, fodder and small timber of the people. These schemes provide for soil conservation, silviculture, horticulture, agro forestry and rehabilitation of degraded forest land. These schemes will mostly benefit Scheduled Caste and Scheduled Tribes. The choice of species has been determined taking into consideration agro climatic condition and choice of the local people. Recommended forest species include Mahua, Tamarind, Neem, Kusum, Sal, Teak, Bahada, Simaruba, Babul, Eucalyptus, Akasia. Besides, horticultural species like jackfruit, mango, cashew, lemon and fodder species like sobabul, sabai grass etc. have been included. Successful implementation of these integrated waste land development projects will go a long way in safeguarding the interests of the tribals. It will bring them prosperity and create more employment opportunities for them. More such schemes should be prepared for the undivided district of Koraput. Only preparation of scheme will not do. What is required is successful implementation of the scheme in close cooperation of the local people.

I may mention about fuel wood and fodder schemes and River Valley Projects which are also under implementation for taking up plantation.

CIDA assisted social forestry programme is in operation in our State. The Project was launched from 1983-84. At the end of December 1993, plantation has been raised over one lakh hectares besides rehabilitation of 34,000 hectares of degraded forest and waste land. Plantation schemes executed by social forestry not only create employment opportunity for the tribals but also meet the fuel wood, fodder and timber and minor forest produce needs of the tribals.

A word about reorientation in the attitude of forest officials will not be out of place. Forests are no longer considered as a source of revenue. It is treated as an asset. Now the accent is on social forestry, conservation of forest, Joint Forest Management and large scale afforestation. The forest officials particularly at the grassroot level are increasingly called upon to discharge the functions of a facilitator. Their regulatory role has been redelegated to the background. They have to play the role of facilitator. I am sure they will live up to the expectation.

Before I conclude I would like to thank the organiser of the Council of Analytical Tribal Studies for giving me this opportunity to share my views with you all. I expect that your deliberations would be rewarding and fruitful.

2

PARAMETERS OF FOREST POLICY FOR TRIBAL DEVELOPMENT
Keynote Address

— *Prof. L.K. Mahapatra*

Forest Habitat and Forest Economy

Since time immemorial forest has been the habitat of the tribal people in all the countries with tribal population. In India almost all the tribal groups are found in their forest habitat, although some of the tribal population may also be found in non-tribal villages, towns and cities. Out of the total population of India the scheduled tribes constitute 7.95 per cent in 1991, compared to 7.83 per cent in 1981 census. Out of the total scheduled tribe population of India (67,758,380), 62,751,026 are rural and 5,007,354 are urban in residence in 1991. The rural scheduled tribes constitute 92.16 per cent of the total scheduled tribe population and the urban scheduled tribes constitute 7.39 per cent only in 1991. In Orissa, out of the total scheduled tribe population of 7,032,214, 94.86 per cent constitute rural inhabitants, only 5.14 per cent are urban. In 1981, Orissa had 95.39 per cent of its scheduled tribe population in rural areas, and 4.61 per cent in urban areas, so the urban scheduled tribes have increased in percentage of the total scheduled tribe population in the decade since 1981. But, the Census figures or any other National Survey do not give the total tribal population residing inside or on the fringe of the forest. However, it is probably not too wide of the mark to estimate forest dwelling tribal population as constituting about 80 per cent of the total scheduled tribe population of Orissa. "Forest dwelling" does not mean that the tribal population resides inside the forest. But, the tribal people residing on the fringe or in the vicinity of the forest, within the daily walking distance from the forest, should be sufficient for our purpose of characterizing them as "forest dwellers".

There are quite a large number of what is known as "forest villages", which have been registered as such with the forest department, which grant them limited rights of occupation of the land identified as forest land. Apart from these forest villages, there are also revenue villages inside even in the reserve forest, where the tribal inhabitants have been issued *ryotwari patta*. On the other hand, there are *ryotwari patta* holders in revenue villages in the Bonda hills of Malkangiri district, which the forest department does not recognize as such, but shows the entire Bonda hills as mixed bamboo forest in the latest map at the Divisional Office at Jeypore, even in 1990. Therefore, although the forest is the habitat of the tribal people in Orissa, as elsewhere, the forest villages and revenue villages on the forest land constitute two different habitat patterns and two different sets of forest rights and forest use.

Forest has always played pivotal role in the economy of the tribal peoples even before historical times. In the colonial period, there was commercialization of forest produce for the first time in a vast scale. Even in the interior regions of Orissa commercial exploitation of the forests go back atleast to 1920's, when companies from outside brought in sawyers into the forests and sleepers for the railways were made and exported. Blocks of the mature forests were auctioned for commercial purposes. Although forest produce was collected and sold in the weekly markets or otherwise by the forest dwelling tribes, the commercialization of minor forest produce is a colonial phenomenon with rise of the *bidi* factories and with large scale distillation of *mahua* spirits by the wine makers. Some minor forest produce assumed disproportionate importance in the economy of the forest dwellers during the colonial period. Use of tobacco and maize, among other things, may have taken roots after the European intrusion, but today everywhere in tribal India one finds tobacco and maize in use. Similarly, when the tribal people are used for decades to depending on collection and sale of minor forest produce, these have entered into their economy as an irreversible component.

Thus, we find tribal hunters and food gatherers, swidden cultivators and pastoralists using the forest since time immemorial as major means of livelihood. But, since the colonial period their utilization of minor forest produce has been a vital link with the outside world economy as also a very important source of cash income as a part of their life support system. There are some tribal groups like *Sahara* or *Sa-ara* in the vicinity of temple towns in ancient Orissa and in recent times, who had the main source of livelihood in cutting fuel wood in the jungle and selling it to the town dwellers and villagers. There are other tribal groups who made charcoal in the forest and sold it to blacksmiths and others as a major means of livelihood. All tribal people residing near the forest or inside the forest used wood and bamboo, and reeds (*chhana*) as building materials. Their cattle and other domestic animals regularly grazed in the forest. Even when, a tribal group is not a hunter and food gatherer, who has to depend on the forest as sole source of livelihood. Other tribal groups including those who live in the vicinity of the forest but practice settled agriculture like *Santal, Munda* etc. also depend on the forest for various food and non-food products including herbal medicines as a matter of their cultural tradition and age old linkages. There are tribal peoples like the *Khadia* in Similipal forest. Who collect and sale honey, arrow-root, sal resin (*jhuna*) and other minor forest produce including mynah birds. In nutshell, the tribal people and the forest as the source of the livelihood and as the place where they mostly reside and prefer to live, are inseparable. Though, there are some evidences or theories or folklore of the tribal people themselves that some tribal people have come to occupy the hills and forests away from their original home in the plains and valleys, their present habitat in or around the forest has been a historical fact for centuries, if not millennia.

In the book on Forests, Environment and Tribal Economy, Walter Fernandes and others have hypothesized that the additional pressure on swidden cultivation is because of the decrease in the supply of Minor Forest Produce (MFP) due to deforestation. In their study in Orissa they find that 13.24 per cent in their sample had mentioned MFP collection as their main occupation and 33.82 per cent as their subsidiary occupation. In other words, 47.06 per cent of their sample had depended on MFP as either their primary or subsidiary occupation. "In an area where job opportunities are few and viable economic alternatives all but non-existent, this dependence is significant, for even subsidiary occupation involves total dependence for survival for at least three lean months in a year". (Fernandes, *et al.,* 1988: 100). They have found that displaced persons from Hirakud Dam Project and from other minor/medium irrigation projects have taken to selling firewood as their main source of livelihood after displacement and self-sponsored resettlement. (*cf. ibid.*: 95-96). It is interesting to note that the displaced people consumed firewood close to the national average of 0.603 kg. coal equivalent per capita per day and sale of firewood was minimum before displacement. This was because they depended on cultivation and sale of MFP other than firewood for their subsistence.

"A recent study regarding the impact of MFP collection on the socio-economic life of tribals conducted by Tribal Research and Training

Institute, Ahmedabad has shown about 35 per cent of the earning of tribals in the Panchamahal District of Gujarat State was from these items. Some other studies also indicate the potential of MFP for tribal economy". (Roy Burman, 1982: 21).

"The tribal communities in India largely occupy forested regions where for long period in their history they have lived in isolation but in harmony with nature. They draw their sustenance largely from the forest. They have had symbiotic relationship with the forest which continues undisturbed in the interior areas even now". (Roy Burman, 1982: 19).

Forest Utilization and Forest Conservation

Forest resources are utilized by modern man not only for his household needs but also for continuing the processes of a complex society, which requires paper for functioning. I need not refer to the story of the *New York Times*, which consumes a big chunk of forest everyday. Especially since independence in India large scale deforestation has occurred either for locating major industries, water management schemes, mining etc. or for commercial purposes. Both the uses require clear felling of the trees. Even in swidden cultivation clear felling is not resorted to. The tree stumps remain and help regenerate the trees from new shoots. Many kinds of trees are spared from burning by the swidden cultivators in their self-interest. Trees yielding edible and non-edible oil, many varieties of food trees, trees on which the silk or tassar worms grow by feeding on the leaves or the tree on which stock lac organisms grow, trees with edible leafs, flowers etc. are left standing in the swiddens. The tribal people persuing food gathering and hunting do not destroy neither the animals and birds' huts nor plant resources wantonly. As a matter of fact, the tribal hunters do not kill wild animals during the period the animals are pregnant. Hence they conserve nature in their own interest. Similarly, the food gatherers leave a portion of the tubers, yams or roots in the ground the tribal dig up for food. Therefore, the tribal people on no account destroy the forest resources, but on the contrary, they conserve the forest resources. Only when in a traumatic situation, for example, under threat of displacement do the tribal people develop a thoroughly destructive attitude towards the forest. (*cf.* Mahapatra 1992). It has been found by the Partially Excluded Areas Committee for Orissa (so-called Thakkarbapa Committee) that the forests in Koraput district managed by the tribal people were in much better condition of growth than the forests managed by the Forest Department under the British government (*cf.* Mahapatra 1990 and 1993). Roy Burman reports that some of the *khuntkatti* communal forests were better managed than the reserved forests under direct management of Forest Department. (Roy Burman, 1986). Mahapatra (1993) refers to "the paradoxical, yet almost comical, situation in Orissa, arising out of the implementation of Orissa Forest Act 1972 and India Forest Act 1927. While village forest under Indian Forest Act is State property, which is placed at the disposal of the village community by the State in the interest of the village, village forest under Orissa Forest Act is primarily communal property, which is deemed to be under the disposal of the State, for the benefit of the community".

To further quote Roy Burman on the issue of community rights for development in Orissa "under the Indian Forest Act, though the village community can manage the forest on being assigned by the State, it cannot attract institutional finance and make investment on its own as the proprietory right vests with the State. Under the Orissa Forest Act, though communal ownership is recognized, as the right of management is taken over by the State, the village community cannot initiate development". On this Mahapatra comments, "the head is won by the State and tail is lost by the village". (*cf.* Mahapatra, 1993).

The Orissa State Gazetteer Volume III (1992) notes very interestingly that "the forests in the ex-princely states were generally well preserved prior to Independence except for some over-fellings during World War II. . . . When the Estate Abolition Act of 1951 was enforced, about 19,942 sq. km. of badly managed ex-zamindary forests came under the Government. . . ."

Those who have seen the bald hills in Koraput district, which was a Zamindary, with the tribes practising swidden cultivation already in 1940's, it becomes difficult for them to visualize the swidden-affected wooded hills of northern ex-princely states of Bonai, Pallahada and Keonjhar in early 1950's. To my mind, this difference in the level of conservation of the forest is due mostly to the communal rights over the forest for swidden cultivation in the northern ex-princely states in contrast with the individual land holding in Jeypore Zamindary in Koraput district. Swidden cultivation has often been blamed for wide scale deforestation. But the real devils are the population pressure and circumscription forest areas because of reservation of the forests near the hill village habitation. As Fernandes notes, there is a "vicious circle of a smaller area available, deforestation, indebtedness and greater dependence of a large number of families on shifting cultivation for survival, leading to another process of deforestation and deterioration of the socio-economic condition of the dwellers". Thus, the cultivation cycle of land-use and fallowing gets reduced to six or seven or three years (*cf.* Fernandes *et al.*, 1988). Fernandes notes in conclusions: "It should be clear from our data that shifting cultivation that destroys forests is a recent phenomenon and is a symbol of a deeper problem". (*ibid.*). Opening of more and more areas of mining and locating development projects in the interior tribal areas have literally driven the tribal swidden cultivators to other areas where swidden cultivation is still practised. Thus, swidden cultivation has always been an unavoidable refuge of the landless, and the displaced immigrant tribal villagers fell back upon swidden cultivation as a means of livelihood wherever village forests were common property resources. (*cf.* Mahapatra, 1960 and 1990).

The tribal swiddeners have been much maligned for soil erosion in the mountainous region and flooding down the hills. Recent research in the more fragile high mountain regions of North India has led scholars to assert that: "There is no evidence of a direct effective linkage between over-exploitation of resources in the mountains and flooding in the foreland . . . . Neither can forests prevent floods after torrential rains. . . . Considering the overall system, erosion caused by anthropogenic factors exerts only an insignificant influence on the processes like flood danger and sedimentation in the foreland, when compared to erosion caused by natural forces. . . . Changes in annual run-off are the result of climatic processes". (*cf.* Kreutzmann, 1993: 52-53). It may be interesting to note that Jack D. Ives and Bruno Messerli have critically examined the so-called "Himalayan Dilemma", which focuses on the environmental degradation, erosion and flooding of the foreland as mainly due to over-population and deforestation on the high mountains. Kreutzmann points to the conclusion reached by the authors of the book: *The Himalayan Dilemma: Reconciling Development and Conservation* (1989, London/New York) in the following paraphrased words: "Population growth and deforestation alone do not present sufficient parameters for the explanation of the "Himalayan Dilemma". Physical phenomena rather find their explanation more in the "normal" surface processes of a mountain range of recent uplift. . . ." (*ibid.*, 53).

Forest villages have been sometimes blamed for forest destruction. It is conveniently forgotten that originally forest villages were established for supply of manpower to help the forest department to exploit forest resources. Forest villages exist under the threat of eviction for failure to fulfil the obligations under which these were established. Roy Burman

Committee has come across a form of agreement between the forest department and the forest village mentioning that the forest department has "the first claim to his labour on payment of reasonable daily wages" and the forest villager is "liable to summary ejectment without compensation by orders of the Divisional Forest Officer for any breach of the terms and conditions" of the agreement, although this runs against the land tenancy laws. (*cf.* Roy Burman, 1982). This Committee recommended conversion of forest villages into normal revenue villages with inalienable ownership rights to land.

Tropical forests in India are a great source of medicinal plants. In the Attapadi valley of Kerala a study of tribal medicine was undertaken by Kerala Forest Research Institute. It found that the local tribal groups used the roots of 39 different species, fruits of 15 species, leaves of 30 species, stems and bark of 12 species each, latex and flowers of 2 species each and the entire plants of 9 species for different medicinal purposes, including treatment of fever, cuts, burns, pain and skin diseases. (KFRI, 1980). This is in addition to abortifants and antifertility preparations. Similar medicinal plants are reported from Gandhamardan hills in Western Orissa and Simlipal hill forest in Northern Orissa.

Forests are increasingly becoming more important as sources of industrial raw materials. Today forest produce support a large number of major and minor industries, such as saw mills, paper, plywood, distillaries hydrogenated oils, polyfibres, match, turpentine, tannins, and drugs etc.

Forest Policy Perspectives

"The enormous potential of forests for contributing to an uplift our rural economy should be viewed in the context of the finding poverty and the country's dual society with the top ten per cent getting most of the benefits of development".

"The gravest problem facing the rural poor is that of lack of productive employment. As Dr. M.S. Swaminathan (1982: 102) remarked, famines in India are not famines of food but of work. There are some 90 million jobless people in India with more than 7 million additional people entering the job market every year. Unfortunately, the pattern of industrialization adopted by us absorbs barely 5 lakhs of these new entrants leaving more than 6.5 million yearly to add to the already enormous pool of unemployed".

As we will explore further, the only possible solution to this famine of work can come from land and water based jobs, which even today employ six times as many people as are employed in industry, trade and government together. Unfortunately, the depletion of our forest resources is now contributing to further destruction of employment and standards of living of the rural poor. Bhatt (1981: 108) has documented that the depletion of bamboo stocks of Tamilnadu has reduced the earnings of basket-weavers from Rs. 8 per day in the early 1970s to less than Rs. 6 per day now. Furthermore, "presently these basket-weavers are always under threat of sudden periods of unemployment of several weeks due to unavailability of bamboos: a situation they had never known till a decade ago". (Gadgil *et al.*,: 1982).

The Planning Commission in its Eighth Plan has made observation in similar vein: "The causes for environmental degradation are many. The prevailing conditions of poverty and underdevelopment themselves create a situation where people are forced to live in squalor and further degrade their environment. On the other hand, the process of development itself may damage the environment, if not properly managed. In the final analysis, removal of poverty, generation of employment, raising the levels of education and increasing awareness of the people are crucial for protection of environment". (Planning Commission, Vol. II, 92).

Forest became a part of the concurrent list by a constitutional Amendment in 1976. Since the beginning of the Fifth Plan period, social forestry schemes have been taken up under the all India policy recommended by the National Commission on Agriculture—Social Forestry Programmes includes mixed plantation, rehabilitation of degraded forests, rural fuel wood plantation, coastal shelter belt plantation, farm forestry etc. As a part of the new 20-point economic programme of the Prime Minister, programmes of afforestation, social and farm forestry were to be pursued vigorously.

Basically Social Forestry is designed to meet the benefits and primary needs of the tribal and rural population as opposed to the needs of industries and the urban elite. The deciderate are: (a) a mixed production system including fruit, fodder, grass, fuel-wood, fibre, small timber etc.; (b) involvement of the beneficiaries right from the planning; (c) minimal government control; (d) financial contribution by local bodies, voluntary contributions, government subsidies; (e) use of communal and Government lands. (*cf.* Roy Burman, 1982.)

The Planning Commission has wisely commended decentralization in power and management over forest in the following lines: "No Government can protect, regenerate and ensure sustainable use of natural resources on its own. It is essential, therefore, to decentralise control over natural resources. Decentralisation, in this context, means transfer of control from the Government to the people collectively. An instance of this is the social forestry programme. For collective control, it is important that conditions should be created for effective management through creation of appropriate local bodies and institutional structure. The people must also have access to information and professional knowledge and must be able to call upon technical bodies for advice and support. Such an approach is even more necessary in the case of tribals and other communities who are traditionally dependent on natural product. A major initiative in decentralising power will be to enable the villagers to decide for themselves their own priorities and to take up activities accordingly. . . ." (Planning Commission, Vol. II: 94). It also clarifies further: "In view of the symbiotic relationship between the tribals and the forest, efforts have been made to associate tribals and other people living in and around forests in general for the protection and development of forests. . . ." (*ibid.*, 98).

The report of the Committee on Forest and Tribals in India, headed by Prof. B.K. Roy Burman, had noted that out of more than 21,000 botanical species reported from forest areas in the country less than 300 species have been important as minor forest produce of some commercial importance. The Roy Burman Committee has recommended that collection of MFP for food and cash income should be conceded as the right of the tribal families without restriction. It is not right to point out that MFP is also important for non-food purposes in the tribal economy, for example, for house construction and grazing. The Committee recommends organized collection and marketing of MFP. It has been estimated that 40 per cent of the MFP resources of the country are located in Madhya Pradesh. We have to find out the MFP resources of other States including Orissa. The Committee finds the most crucial problem of marketing has been rather neglected. Remunerative price to the tribal collector for MFP can make significant contribution to his subsistence economy, as it insists. In many areas in central India it has been noted that, wherever there has been State monopoly for purchase of MFP from the tribal people, they have usually been either cheated or denied the fair price for MFP, and most often a price lower than the prevailing market price. This has been, the findings of my study in the two most backward Gram Panchayats namely, Belghar in Phulbani district and Bholagadia in Mayurbhanj district (*cf.* Mahapatra, 1982-83). The Committee recommends scientific and discriminating utilization of MFP and there marketing through co-operatives in which the tribal people have the dominant say.

Realizing the importance of forest-based industries for the tribal people, yet also taking note of the constrains of the tribal people, Roy Burman Committee recommended that a forest-based industry should be a "joint venture of the three parties i.e., the concerned corporation, the entrepreneur and the tribal producer and collector of raw materials". The Corporations here refer to State-level Forest Development Corporation or Tribal Development Corporation etc. Processing of MFP for value-addition at the primary society (e.g., LAMPS) level is necessary to bring direct benefit to the tribal collectors, most of whom are women and children.

Financial institutions have been proverbially shy in coming to tribal areas for supporting plantations of villagers as a resource or raw materials asset for industry. As some of the tribal groups like the Hill Bonda, the Saora or the Dongiriya Kondh have clan or lineage territories as their common property resources, such corporate bodies are difficult to be recognized as legal '*persons*' for commercial contracts. But if we want the tribal people to retain and develop their "genius", we have to accept certain structural entities not familiar to capitalistic commercial institutions.

Roy Burman Committee raises a vital issue on the forest management system. It says, "the crux of the problem of forest management lies in the need for integration of tribal and forest economies. The present atmosphere of confrontation between tribals and foresters should be transferred into one of cooperation and partnership. The human factors has been neglected in forest management which has been oriented predominantly towards forest practices. There are three salient desiderata. In the first place, an identify-interest between the forest Departments and the people (notably tribals) should be created. Secondly, the development programmes should aim at internalising its various components into the rural production system as a whole. Thirdly, the management should ensure strong backward and forward linkages between forestry and other development sectors on the local, regional State and national levels". (Roy Burman, 1982).

The forest administrators and conservators should not always look upon forest as a merely revenue generating sector. Forests provide much needed inputs to the rural sector in the form of fuelwood, construction materials, fodder etc. which do not appear as revenue to the State. "It is nevertheless a real economic benefit to the society as a whole". (Gadgil *et al.*, 1982). Let us examine one example for what it is worth.

"Gujarat, with only about 5 per cent of its area under-effective forest cover and famous for its enterprising businessman and farmers, has launched the most innovative social forestry programme of all" (Karamchandani, 1982). There were several components to this programme such as strip plantations along roadsides, canal banks and railway lines with village panchayats promised 50 per cent of the net profits on maturity. By 1981, some 2000 village woodlots have been created covering 17,000 hectares. The lots are raised at Government expense, but the panchayat will receive 50 per cent of net profits on maturity.

This highly imaginative programme involves landless families in the planting and protecting operations in a manner that ensures them both a regular income and a share in the net profit from the harvest. Each family is assigned 37.5 ha. of degraded forest to be planted at the rate of 2.5 ha/year over a period of 15 years. Each family is committed to provide 40 mandays of work a month and in return is paid a fixed monthly remuneration of Rs. 250, housing materials free of charge, minor forest produce and 20 per cent of the net profit from the harvest at the end of 15 years.

The innovative programme encourages farmers to put degraded and marginal farmland under tree crops by furnishing free seedlings and an additional subsistence allowance of Rs. 250 per year, provided that the survival is above 70 per cent. A modification of this programme has been applied to the tribal tract in the Dangs.

"By 1980, 605 farmers had taken to planting eucalyptus and obtained yields of well over 20 tonnes/ha/year on irrigated land replacing cotton, leading to net annual profit of Rs. 6,000 to Rs. 10,000 per hectare". (Gadgil *et al.*, 1982.)

Tribal swiddeners have realized that they have to change their technology and diversify their economy in order to live and thrive in the modern world. Even the Hill Bonda, a primitive tribe in Southern Orissa, and the Pauri Bhuiyan and the Juang, other primitive tribes of Northern Orissa, have always tried to construct terraces in the bed of the hill streams, where feasible. But such locations are scarce and terrace making is not only arduous, but also costly in time and in lost opportunities to earn their daily bread, while they work on several operations connected with terrace construction, often extending over two generations. Much as the Hill Bonda and Hill Saora are masters in such terrace construction both in the hill stream bed, as also on dry upland, they find to their horror and distress, that the terraced land cannot be recorded as their private property, not because it is their clan or lineage land. Either the land is above 10 per cent slope,—and the land settlement officials are not empowered to get this land recorded as privately cultivated land with *ryotwari* rights, or the Forest Department claims the land as under some category of forest and thus cannot be diverted to non-forest use and recorded as land under cultivation, as per the Forest Conservation Act of 1980. Fortunately, the present Chief Minister of Orissa has decreed that in Kashipur Block/Tahsil of Rayagada sub-division the tribal people be given property rights in cultivated land—as terraces, swiddens or upland upto 30° slope. When the tribal people are in actual possession of land for cultivation even above 30° slope, either in the form of swidden or otherwise, they shall be regarded as *raiyats* for this land, provided the land beyond 30° slope is utilized for raising perennial crops in the form of plantations etc. This conditional grant of rights will be entered in the *patta*, so that in case of violation of the condition, the rights of *raiyat* may be revoked. That means, the tribal swiddeners in Kashipur can either grow perennial tree crops or raise a forest on hill slopes beyond 30° and the fruits and the yield from these tree will be theirs, and not of the Forest Department. In this way, the Chief Minister has stuck down at one stroke all the restrictions imposed by the Revenue and Forest Departments on the tribal *raiyat* to own trees as exclusive possession above 30° slope.

In this way, ecological considerations have been met, economic well-being of the tribal people has been ensured and the age-old process of depriving the tribal people of the hardwon fruits of their back-breaking labour, that is, the terraces and cultivated fields beyond 10° slope has been reversed. Under this dispensation, the poorest landless tribal families, who do not have any permanent fields may at least "own" the swiddens and trees and get adequate compensation as raiyats and tree-owners even above 30° slope, in the event of displacement. As the Departments of Revenue and Forests have accepted this trend-setting decision in respect of Kashipur tribal groups, it is expected that this will be agreed to in respect of other swidden cultivation areas in Orissa. Once Orissa shows the way, other States with swidden cultivation and exclusive rights over trees among tribal groups, namely, Madhya Pradesh, Andhra Pradesh, Karnataka and Assam and other north-eastern States are also expected to grant such rights to their tribal people. Of course, where the Sixth Schedule of the Constitution operates and village common property resources are managed by the local people, the forest is conserved and developed in the interest of the tribal people. (*cf.* Mahapatra, 1994).

In support of the above mentioned decision of the Government of Orissa we may take into consideration one important ecological situation for appreciating the significance of agricultural practices in checking soil erosion on mountain slopes. Modern research on the mountainous regions of North India has established that "Forest clearance on steep slopes...can have the effect of a reduction in soil erosion, if terracing for agricultural purposes takes place, which is a characteristic of many regions of the mountain arc. The human factor is, therefore, by no means only a negative one, landslide zones, too, are stabilized by the very fact of terracing. . . ." (Kreutzmann, 1993: 53).

Enlightened and humane forest policy should see to it that the forest is to serve the people and provide their needs; if the people are denied their legitimate dues and rights, they will not protect the forest, but will destroy it with as much unconcern as the forest conservators trample down the people's needs and rights with unconcern. If it is necessary to break the nexus between Veerappan-forester-politician in the interest of the nation, it is also equally necessary to foster and develop the nexus of people-forester-politician in the interest of the nation. Already enlightened foresters are eiding the forest protection and management by the people in the villages as in Gujarat villages. (*cf.* R.S. Pathan, N.J. Arul, M. Poffenberger, S.K. Dhar, J.R. Gupta, and Madhu Sarin; Shashi Kant, Neera Mendirata and Kundan Kumar). These foresters have come to realise the wise saying that it is better to have half a loaf than lose one. Instead of motivating people to protect their forest—*their forest*, if the forest department alienates and disinherits them from their traditional rights and economic base, the result would be what has happened in Bonda Hills: the forest exists on paper and maps of the Forest Department but not in the Bonda Hills. Similarly, about 19.47 per cent of the total geographical area of India is under actual forest cover, although the country has an area of 752.3 lakh hectares (23%) notified as forest as per India 1992, a Government of India publication. But the credibility gap between the nominal forest cover and the actual forest cover is much wider in Orissa State compared to India as a whole. For, in Orissa 59,963 sq. km, or 38.48 per cent of the total land surface are supposed to be under the forest cover whereas the satellite imagery pictures do not credit Orissa with even 20 per cent of the total land surface under actual forest cover. Because of the over-jealous implementation of the 1980

Forest Conservation Act in Orissa many tribal communities have become impoverished, malnourished and disease-ridden, so much so that the middle-age population look haggard and emaciated and meet premature death. This has happened, among others, in the Pauri Bhuiyan villages of Bonai in Mahulpada region, which I visited in 1989. The Forest Department had drawn its Reserved Forest line so close to the revenue village on the hills that the swiddener hill community was left with no means and resources—land, forest and technology—to maintain their precarious physical survival.

Specific Recommendations for Reformulating Forest Policy

Roy Burman Committee (1982) has recommended that:

(i) The traditional rights, concessions and privileges of tribals in respect of all forest produce, grazing and hunting should not be abridged. They should be freely allowed to visit places of their worship inside the forests. Further, they should be suitably recorded.

(ii) In the forest villages, they should be given heritable and inalienable right over the land which they cultivate.

(iii) There should be restriction on deforestation of the area vulnerable to soil erosion, landslide, desertification etc. Felling of fruit trees should, ordinarily, be prohibited.

(iv) Association of tribal should be ensured in a large scale plantation programme giving them the right to usufruct.

(v) Ownership right on the trees growing in the holding allotted to a tribal in a forest village should vest in him.

(vi) National parks, sanctuaries, bio-sphere should normally be not located close to the tribal villages. Persons displaced on account of their creation should be properly rehabilitated.

(vii) There should be attempt at simplification of laws and procedures so that tribals can comprehend them.

(viii) Relevant laws should be modified so that the village councils can obtain term-loan against standing tree-stock in forests.

(ix) If necessary, the State might assume the right to provide guidelines about land-use and resource-mobilization on communal, clan and private lands. The operation of the Bill framed by the Government of Orissa aimed at restriction of sale of timber trees belonging to tribals might be watched for adoption by other State Governments.

To these recommendations we may add, in line with the National Forest Policy, 1988: "The holders of customary rights and concessions in forest areas should be motivated to identify themselves with protection and development of forests from which they derive benefits", the following recommendations are being acted upon:

(x) The Government should grant the *raiyati* rights to swidden cultivators upto 30° slope, if these lands are under cultivation as terraces, upland permanent dryfields or as swiddens, and beyond 30° slope, if these lands are under permanent tree crops as orchards or forest on the model of Orissa's Status Rule for Survey and Settlement Operation in Kashipur Tahsil of Koraput (now Malkangiri) district as revised in Letter No. 20321 dated 10.4.92 from the Revenue and Excise Department addressed to the Director of Land Records and Surveys, Board of Revenue, Orissa (See Appendix).

(xi) The Reserve Forest around revenue villages in Orissa and elsewhere, as also around Forest villages, should be re-demarcated in view of (x) above to provide reasonable common property resources (land, forest, water bodies), so that the food gatherers, hunters and swiddener communities may be *rehabilitated in situ* in the hills and secure other amenities to improve their quality of life. (*cf.* Mahapatra, 1994).

The Planning Commission's directive is very clear and should be adhered to in reformulation of the national policy on forest and other natural resources : "An important task before the Government is the formulation of a comprehensive national policy on nature and natural resources. To be effective it must be evolved in consultation with the people. The policy must also spell out the position regarding environmental needs of the society in general and the rights of the weaker sections such as, tribals, nomads, women and children, especially in terms of giving access to and control over natural resources in particular". (Planning Commission, 1992-94).

APPENDIX

Extract from the letter No. 20321 dt. 10.4.92 from Deputy Secretary to Government, Revenue & Excise Department addressed to the Director of Land Records & Surveys, Board of Revenue, Orissa, Cuttack.

Sub: Status Rule for Survey and Settlement Operation in Kashipur Tahsil of Koraput District.

Ref: Government letter Nos. (a) 41777/R, dated 15.7.1989 (b) 49830/R, dated 4.8.1989 and (c) No. 17181/R, dated 15.4.1991.

In inviting a reference to the letters on the subject cited above, I am directed to say that in this Department G.O. No. 17181/R dated 15.4.1991 referred to above, instructions were issued that Donger Khasara shall be prepared in favour of tribal persons doing Donger cultivation on the hill slopes beyond 10°. It was stipulated in the G.O. among other things that the land in respect of which Donger Khasara should be prepared had to be utilized for agro-forestry purpose.

2. In modification of the aforesaid Government orders, it has been decided that *raiyati* right shall be conferred on the tribals who are in cultivating possession of the hill slopes either in form of Pudu or Kudki upto 30°.

3. Tribals in cultivating possession of the hill slopes above 30° either in form of Kudki or Podu or otherwise shall also be recorded as *raiyats* in respect of such land. Conferment of such right is subject to the provision that the land beyond 30° slope shall only be utilized for raising perennial crops in the form of plantations etc. In the remarks column of the *patta* to be issued in such case, the condition that the land is meant for raising perennial crops in the form of plantations and in the event of failure to do so the right of conferred in respect of such land be revoked, shall be recorded.

4. Transfer of any land to be settled in the manner indicated in para 2 and 3 above is not permissible except by way of mortgage in favour of any public financial institution for securing a loan granted by such institution for any agricultural purpose. The settlement shall be cancelled for violation of this condition. This condition shall be appropriately recorded in the remarks column of the *patta*.

5. In view of the above, you are requested to take action accordingly.

REFERENCES

Bhatt, S.R., 1981, *Problems of the Management of Bamboo Resources in Tamilnadu*, Indian Institute of Management, Bangalore (Mimeographed).

Dhar, S.K. and J.R. Gupta, *Participatory Forest Management in the Shivalik Hills*. Sustainable Forest Management Working Paper No. 5, Ford Foundation.

Fernandes, Walter; Geeta Menon and Philip Viegas, 1988, *Forests, Environment and Tribal Economy*, Indian Social Institute, New Delhi.

Gadgil, Madhav; S. Narendra Prasad and Rauf Ali, 1983, Forest Management and Forest Policy in India : A Critical Review in *Forests, Environment and People* (ed), Walter Fernandes. Indian Social Institute, New Delhi.

Government of Orissa, 1992, *Orissa State Gazetteers*, Vol. III.

Government of India, 1993, India 1992, Ministry of Information and Broadcasting, New Delhi.

Kant, Shashi; Neera Mendirata and Kundan Kumar, 1990, *Community Forest Management in Orissa, Workshop on Sustainable Forestry*, Ford Foundation, New Delhi.

Karamchandani, K.P., 1982, *Extensions, Components, Social Forestry, Gujarat*, Gujarat Forest Department, Vadodara.

KFRI, 1980, *Studies on the Changing Patterns of Man—Forestry Interaction and Its Implications on Ecology and Management*, Kerala Forest Research Institute, Trivandrum.

Kreutzmann, H., 1993, *Development Trends in the High Mountain Regions of the Indian Subcontinents: A Review* in Applied Geography and Development, Vol. 42, Institute for Scientific Cooperation, Turbingen.

Mahapatra, L.K., 1960, *A Hill Bhuiyan Village*, Hamburg University, (Mimeographed).

Mahapatra, L.K., 1982-1983, Barriers to Development in Isolated Tribal Areas: Two Case Studies of Most Backward Gram Panchayats in Orissa, in *Manav*, Vol. I, No. 1.

Mahapatra, L.K., 1990, *Rehabilitation of Tribals Affected by Major Dams and Other Projects in Orissa* in Workshop on Rehabilitation of Persons Displaced by Development Projects (ed), A.P. Fernandes, Institute for Social and Economic Change, Bangalore.

Mahapatra, L.K., 1992, *Development for Whom? Depriving the Dispossessed Tribals* in National Development and Tribal Deprivation (ed.) Walter Fernandes, Indian Social Institute, New Delhi.

Mahapatra, L.K., 1993, *Customary Rights in Land and Forest and the State* in Continuity and Change in Tribal Society (ed.) M. Miri, Indian Institute of Advanced Study, Shimla.

Mahapatra, L.K., 1994, *Tribal Development in India: Myth and Reality*, Vikas, New Delhi.

Pathan, R.S.; N.J. Arul and M. Poffenberger, *Forest Protection Committees in Gujarat—Joint Management Initiative Sustainable Forest Management*, Working Paper No. 7.

Planning Commission, 1992, *Eighth Five Year Plan (1992-97)*, Vol. II, Government of India.

Roy Burman, B.K., 1982, *Report of Committee on Forest and Tribals in India*, Tribal Development Division, Ministry of Home Affairs, New Delhi.

Roy Burman, B.K., 1986, *Historical Ecology of Land Survey and Settlement in Tribal Areas and Challenges of Development*, Council for Social Development, New Delhi.

Swaminathan, M.S., 1982, *Irrigation and Our Agricultural Future*, A.N. Khosla Memorial Lecture, New Delhi.

3

FOREST POLICY OF ORISSA
A Third Visit

— *N.C. Sahu* and *B.N. Das*

Preamble

The authors considered Orissa's forest policy in 1979 (29); then they had a second look at it in 1983 (30). Now there are compelling reasons to re-re-consider it.

The Setting

There have occurred significant changes in the approach towards the economic-ecologic system at the global, national and regional levels, The question of the feasibility, necessity and desirability of economic growth is raised by Boulding,[2] Mishan,[21, 22] Schumachar[33, 34] and Meadows *et al.*,[20] in the late 1960s and early 1970s. In this context physical and psychic survival of the humankind has surfaced as a major issue. As a consequence, the forest policies have now hinged on human-nature symbiosis. Neither the market nor the government fully captures the economic and ecological externalities of the mis-use of forest, which is a common property resource.[1, 32] The need for avoiding the failures and recombining the two basic modes of resource allocation has emerged as very significant. In India, it has been felt that forests should not be looked upon as a revenue earning resource.[9] In the new National Forest Policy of 1988 the focus has shifted to environmental stability. At the regional level, community protection receives attention as the new strategy to combat ecological degradation of the forest-tribal and rural-economy of Orissa. Social forestry is being pushed as people's movement. The ecological steady-state threshold of our forest has to accommodate promotion of economic well being of the common mass.[38] This is the crux of the problem of sustainable development. There has been a paradigm shift in understanding human-forest interaction and relation. While scanning through forest policy of Orissa, we also try to see to what extent the new concerns find their place in it.

Evaluation

Forest policy refers to the body of implicitly assumed and explicitly stated principles which underlie decisions and actions of people and persons who act on forests. In order to fulfil the basic objectives of society, the policies influence the course of development of forests, which are a very vulnerable renewable resource.[31] We try to evaluate such actions and decisions. The criteria cover size, spread, yield, forest as habitat and so on.

Size and Spread

The forest of Orissa were unified combining the parts of the erstwhile Province of Bihar and Orissa, ex-Princely States and ex-Zamindars through a long process which continue until 1957.[6] After the process was complete, the State's forest area stood at about 66 lakh ha. in the records. After a deceptive rising trend[31] until mid 1970s, the reported forest area tapered down (Table 3.1). Against people's privileges, shifting cultivation, encroachments and illicit removals, a cautious view should have been taken from the very beginning. The ex-Zamindary areas were forests only by name. Such areas, designated as Undemarcated Protected Forest (UDPF), had a very poor management record, being "exploited most irregularly with the object of raising maximum revenue".[10] It is only the remote sensing estimations which drew attention since 1970s to the fact that the actual forest cover is 7 to 12 lakh ha less than the recorded figures (Table 3.1). Among other things, the forest richness syndrome created laxity in Orissa to determine the optimum land-use balance. As a result, not only the forest base has shrunk, but also the future possibility of reclothing the UDPF stretching over about 14 lakh ha[17] has almost eroded along with its top soil.

The Map. 3.1 and Table 3.2 testify that the geographic distribution of forests is highly skewed in Orissa. Balasore, Cuttack and Bolangir (undivided) districts have less than 12 per cent of land area under forests. Steps have not been adequately taken to raise fuelwood forests in these districts. Ecological restoration warrants that the grasslands should be protected and waste lands should be brought under some kind of forest vegetation. In Balasore and Sambalpur, there is a small rise in

TABLE 3.1 : Recorded and Actual Forest Area in Orissa during Selected Years

(*ha.* × 10^5)

Sl. No.	*Legal status/ density class*	*1957-58*	*1975-76*	*1981-82*	*1990-91*
1	*2*	*3*	*4*	*5*	*6*
Recorded Forest Land					
1.	Reserved	22.46	26.00	25.04	27.09
2.	Protected*	43.16	41.68	34.92	30.09
3.	Total	65.62	67.68[a]	59.96	57.18[b]
Actual Forest Cover (remote sensing)					
1.	Dense (Density 40 to 100 per cent)	—	34.35	28.57	27.35
2.	Open (Density 10 to 40 per cent)	—	20.85	24.59	19.85
3.	Total	—	55.20	53.16	47.21

* Includes reserved lands, protected lands, ex-Zamindary, Lakhraj, Debottar and Unclassed forests.

a Relates to 1977-78.

b Relates to 1989-90.

Source: 17 and 31.

TABLE 3.2 : District-wise Forest Area in Orissa, 1965 and 1991

(*ha.* × 10^5)

Sl. No.	*Name of district*	*1965*		*1991*		
		Recorded forest area	*Col. 3 as % of land area*	*Actual forest cover (satellite survey)*	*Col. 5 as % of land area*	*Col. 5 as % of Col. 3*
1	*2*	*3*	*4*	*5*	*6*	*7*
1.	Balasore	0.35	5.4	0.37	5.9	105.7
2.	Bolangir	1.83	20.7	1.07	12.0	58.5
3.	Cuttack	1.33	12.2	1.06	9.5	79.7
4.	Dhenkanal	5.85	53.5	3.67	33.9	62.7
5.	Ganjam	6.05	49.4	4.70	37.4	77.7
6.	Kalahandi	3.65	31.5	2.77	23.5	75.9
7.	Keonjhar	4.13	49.5	3.73	44.9	90.3
8.	Koraput	16.26	59.8	7.31	27.1	45.0
9.	Mayurbhanj	4.78	45.9	4.06	39.0	84.9
10.	Phulbani	9.03	81.4	5.96	53.9	66.0
11.	Puri	3.52	33.6	2.33	22.8	66.2
12.	Sambalpur	5.86	33.4	6.17	35.2	105.3
13.	Sundargarh	5.53	56.3	4.01	41.3	72.5
	Total	68.17	43.7	47.21	30.3	69.3

Source : 4, 11 and 17.

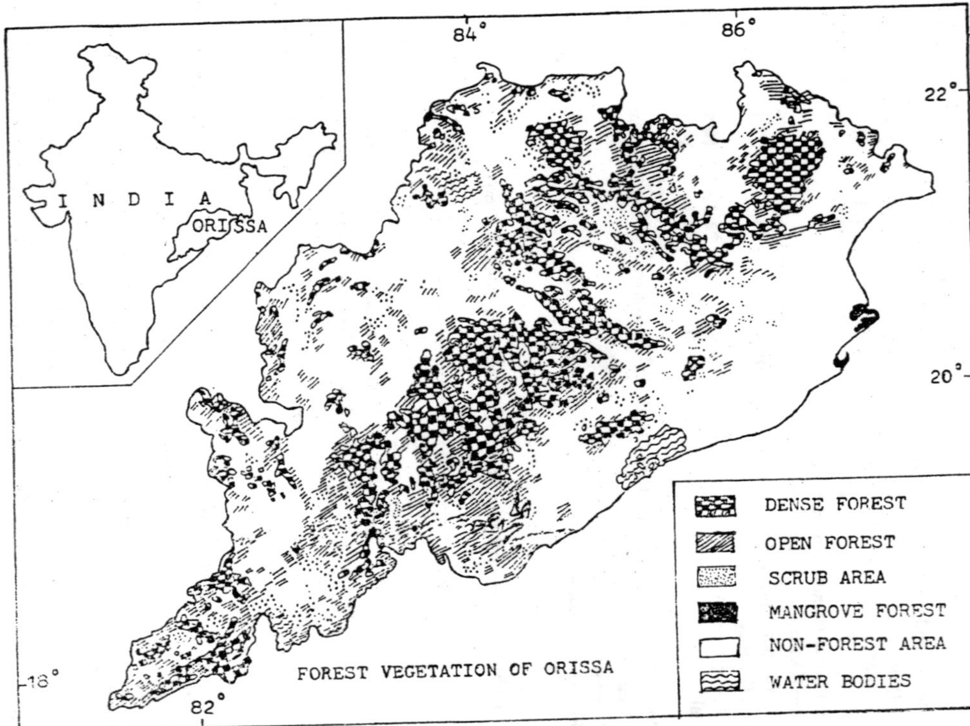

Map. 3.1 : Forest Vegetation of Orissa

Source : National forest vegetation map : Orissa, Forest Survey of India. In : Government of Orissa, 1990. Orissa forests (brochure). Principal CCF, Bhubaneswar.

forest cover. If this is free from estimation errors through satellite imagery, this is a welcome trend which has to be intensified. Over the two decades-and-a-half from 1965, the loss of forests is the highest (55%) in Koraput. In other districts, the loss forest cover vary between 10 and 42 per cent. It is unfortunate that the tribal ecosystems of Koraput, Phulbani and Ganjam have lost so much of forests. In a counter measure, the Government of Orissa imposed ban on commercial exploitation in Bolangir, Kalahandi and Phulbani in 1988 and Ganjam and Koraput in 1990. The total area closed to utilisation except for bamboo, is nearly 29 lakh ha[17] which is more than half of the State's recorded forests. It is believed that the move would protect the socio-cultural milieu and environmental state of the region. The intentions are sound. However, given the age-old conflict between people and government concerning forests, the ban makes the wound burn more. The move should have come out of popular and political emotion, in the absence of which the measure is looked upon as coercion from above.[3] As a result, clandestine removals from the ban areas are the common headlines of our newspapers now-a-days.

Table 3.3 contains information on the conversion of forest land for non-forest purposes. From 1948 to 1991, a total of 1.86 lakh ha. of forest area has been officially disforested for various developmental purposes. Irrigation is the largest claimant of forest land. The rate of disforestation has slowed down over the last four decades. In the 1980s, the significant fall in conversion is attributable to the national Forest Conservation Act, 1980, which has made the process very strict making the approval of the central government mandatory condition.[7, 8] Against official disforestation, new plantation and afforestation have been done over about 6.53 lakh ha. of forest lands (Table 3.4). The official forest creation is 3.5 times higher than disforestation. But more than half of the plantations has been raised only during the 1980s. Also the old man-created forests are in a dubious state. Teak plantations have not been properly thinned and maintained. Moreover, the plantations raised during the first two five-year plans which should have been matured now, have been declared by experts to be a failure for all practical purposes as done in a "very half hazard manner".[24] The plantation ecosystems have the weaknesses associated with monoculture. Given the intergenerational irresponsibility, no amount of man-made forests can fully compensate the value of the natural stock. The ability to listen to the voice of future generations has to be created. Private production forestry needs encourage-ment in Orissa.

TABLE 3.3 : Forest Area Disforested for Non-forest Purposes, 1948 to 1990

(ha × 10^3)

Sl. No.	*Purpose*	*1948-60*	*1960-70*	*1970-80*	*1980-90*	*Total*
1.	Irrigation	90.76	45.86	8.79	4.91	150.32
2.	Industry and Mining	0.35	2.18	0.40	1.54	4.47
3.	Roads	—	—	0.01	0.20	0.21
4.	Railways	2.33	0.02	0.07	0.90	3.32
5.	Others	2.18	6.78	12.84	6.18	27.98
6.	Total	95.62	54.84	22.11	13.73	186.30
7.	Annual rate of disforestation	7.97	5.48	2.21	1.37	—

Source : 12, 13, 14, 17 and 31.

TABLE 3.4 : Plantation Effort in Orissa upto 1989-90

Sl. No.	*Period*	*Plantation* ha × 10^3	*Rehabilitation* ha × 10^3	*Avenue Plantation* Rkm × 10^3	*Seedling Distribution* No × 10^{-}
1	*2*	*3*	*4*	*5*	*6*
1.	Upto 1951-52	32.95	—	—	—
2.	1951-56	0.75	—	—	—
3.	1956-61	7.10	0.52	—	—
4.	1961-66	39.74	7.79	—	—
5.	1966-71	53.67	3.20	—	—
6.	1971-76	47.08	1.34	—	—
7.	1976-81	90.61	11.86	2.68	0.32
8.	1981-86	175.64	61.19	2.71	5.84
9.	1986-90 (4 years)	205.19	140.31	5.87	6.82
	Total	652.73	226.21	11.26	12.98

Source : 12, 13, 14, 17 and 31.

Social forestry is pushed as a movement to reverse the downhill environmental trend in the countryside since 1983. The Orissa Social Forestry Project receives massive assistance from the Swedish International Development Agency. It is an endeavour for creation of common property forest resources for the people and by the people with government support.[26] It essentially involves a strategy of people's participation as individuals and as members of local communities in village forestry activities for rural development and poverty alleviation. In the first (1983-88) and second (1988-93) phases of the project, a total area of about 1.01 lakh ha. has been planted under various schemes covering 7915 villages upto 1990-91. Under farm forestry, 11.23 crores seedlings have been distributed.[17] Out of the woodlots created, about 15 thousand ha. has been notified as village forest in accordance with the Orissa Village Forest Rules, 1985 as amended in 1989.[15]

Forests and Biodiversity Protection

Table 3.5 shows that over the last two decades the detected forest offences have significantly declined. This is contrary to the truth if one considers that the illicit removals from forests, particularly headloads of firewood, has been a common practice throughout the country. This is some kind of self-employment which has been considered as a growing human problem in India arising out of increasing population, acute scarcity of firewood and unemployment. "The foresters have been closing their eyes" towards the illicit part of this activity, considering it as the "goodwill cost of protecting forests".[25] One modest estimate suggests that every year Rs. 100 crores worth of clandestine removals take place from our forests,[24] which is around half the contributions of the forestry and logging sector to the State income (Net State Domestic Product) of Orissa at Current Prices in 1988-89.[18]

TABLE 3.5 : Forest Offence Cases in Orissa, 1971-72 to 1989-90

Sl. No.	*Year*	*No. of cases × 10^3*			*Compensation Realised (Rs. × 10^5)*
		Detected	*Prosecuted*	*Compounded*	
1		*2*	*3*	*4*	*5*
1.	1971-72	47.66	2.70	46.48	9.85
2.	1976-77	42.40	5.09	48.91	14.83
3.	1981-82	62.44	2.83	45.84	39.32
4.	1986 87	29.58	1.68	15.34	12.16
5.	1987-88	29.62	2.17	16.30	12.24
6.	1988-89	33.01	2.42	18.07	11.69
7.	1989-90	12.52	2.90	18.56	14.72

Source : 14 and 17.

In order to contain the above problem, a scheme is being implemented since late 1980s in which the rural community is directly involved in the urgent and enormous task of protecting the reserved and protected forests.[17] The scheme entrusts the responsibility of fire-fighting and prevention of illicit removals and encroachments in the adjoining forest to the protection committees formed in each village and provides for enjoyment of certain usufructs by the people free of cost to meet their requirements of small timber, bamboo and firewood only for household consumption. Under this scheme 6085 village Forest Protection Committees (VFPC)—5654 for reserved forests and 431 for protected forest have been formed in Orissa upto 1991.[17] The area entrusted to the committees is about 14 lakh ha., which is around a quarter of the recorded forest area. It includes about 12 lakh ha. of reserved forests. The scheme is in operation at the instance of the Government of India which has been prescribed in the National Forest Policy, 1988. The scheme has a wise rationale. But like the ban on commercial exploitation, it reflects a thought imposed from above, rather than based on ground reality or research findings. Of course, in certain instances like Binjigiri in Puri, Rupabalia in Dhenkanal and some blocks in Phulbani district the non-governmental organisations (NGOs) have successfully translated the ideal of forest socialism into operational principles.[19] However, this cannot be generalised about the formally structured VFPCs. Moreover, given the frequent newspaper reports on surreptitious felling and poaching, one suspects if mass emotion exists for forest protection in Orissa. Even sanctuaries are not spared as is evident from the reports in *The Prajatantra* dated 17.9.1993 on Similipal. The Sambad dated 23.9.1993 on Lakhari valley,*The Prajatantra* dated 5.10.1993 on Debrigarh and so on.

Forests have suffered too much from the free rider problem. Normal economic rationality prompts an individual to use the common property for private gain. The present economic pressures push wider issues like intergenerational equity and ecological sustainability beyond the ken of an individual. Using surrogate market techniques it has been estimated that the annual rental value of the environmental services such as production of oxygen, conversion to animal protein, soil conservation and maintenance of soil fertility, recycling of water and control of humidity, sheltering of fauna and flora, control of air pollution, safe keeping of biodiversity and outdoor recreation is Rs. 9887 per hectare of forest in 1988-89. This is far higher than the per hectare State revenue and State income values calculated at Rs. 125 and Rs. 433 respectively.[23] The political parties in general and the NGOs in particular have to arouse mass consciousness educating people on the total economic-ecologic value of forests comprising of direct and indirect use values, option value and existence value.[28] Until then, the Forest Department has to closely monitor the community protection programme with extreme caution and elaborate care.

The quality of our natural forests is not very rich, also not very poor. Excepting the semi-evergreen patches in Puri, Koraput and Kalahandi districts, and the tidal (mangrove) forests of Bhitarakanika, about 94 per cent of our forests fall within the tropical moist and dry deciduous types.[31] In the natural stock a large number of species is considered suitable only for firewood and charcoal.[31] The tropical forests are known in the world for rich biodiversity.[37] A composite flora comprising of shrubs, herbs, bamboos, small timber and giant tree species characterise such forests. However, for more than a century the working plans for scientific management of forests tend the stock to retain the commercially important species.[24] Ecological principles have to be integrated with economic working plans.

One important dimension of biodiversity covers wild life. Alongside the shrinking forest base, the wildlife heritage is fast sinking. For preservation and propagation of the faunal wealth of 595 species (65 mammals, 84 reptiles and 446 birds), 15 sanctuaries, one game reserve and one zoological park have been constituted.[17] The Government of Orissa has notified its intention to constitute two national parks in Similipal and Bhitarakanika which are sanctuaries from 1979 and 1975 respectively. But the final approval of the union government is awaited since 1980 for the former and 1988 for the latter. The total area under nature conservation of all wildlife reserves is 7.25 lakh ha. which constitutes about 13 per cent of the State's recorded forests. The Forest Department has proposed to constitute five more sanctuaries at Karlapat (Kalahandi), Kandhakambera, Balimela and Narayanpatna (Koraput) and Gahirmatha marine ecosystem (Cuttack) over an area of 1.84 lakh ha.[17] In these cases, the State Government has not yet notified them as sanctuaries. Delay in legally constituting the nature reserves has caused enormous damage to our forest and faunal wealth. Table 3.6 shows that in case of 8 sanctuaries, legal notification was delayed for as long a period as between 10 and 15 years. The ecosystems of Raigoda, Kapilasa and Saptasajya (Dhenkanal), Padmatola (Phulbani) and Karlapat (Kalahandi) which were declared as sanctuaries by the Forest Department could never be constituted so in the statutes. In the 1980s, the State could not manage to make Similipal an international biosphere reserve. The successes in respect of crocodile and tiger conservation, and captive breeding of several types of wild animals including white tigers from normal coloured parents in Nandankanan are encouraging. The State's wild fauna has very little future under the principle of multiple use forestry. To the extent ecological forestry is important, all representative eco-units be brought under some or other type of nature reserve.

TABLE 3.6 : Time Lag in Notification of Some Sanctuaries in Orissa

Sl. No.	*Name of sanctuary*	*Name of district*	*Year of declaration by Forest Department*	*Year of State government notification*	*Time gap (years)*
1	*2*	*3*	*4*	*5*	*6*
1.	Debrugarh	Sambalpur	1932	1985	53
2.	Balukhand	Puri	1935	1984	49
3.	Chandaka	Puri	1935	1982	47
4.	Raigada	Dhenkanal	1938	—	—
5.	Mahanadi and Baisipalli	Puri-Phulbani	1962	1981	19
6.	Padmatola	Phulbani	1962	—	—
7.	Khalasuni	Sambalpur	1962	1982	20
8.	Ushakoti	Sambalpur	1962	1987	25
9.	Karlapat	Kalahandi	1969	—	—
10.	Similipal	Mayurbhanj	1969	1979	10
11.	Kapilash	Dhenkanal	1970	—	—
12.	Saptasajya	Dhenkanal	1970	—	—

Source : 17 and 31.

On the basis of dominant use principle, ecological, social land production forestry attend to the principal functions of the forest resources.[5] One possible balance is to classify the State's forests equally among three categories, and manage them separately. Necessary rearrangement in the forest organisation can be made. A mere renaming of the Forest Department by Environment and Forest Department does not break the ice. In future, through research studies, and socio-economic-political debate on the issue a better optimum than the one suggested above can emerge. For this to happen, the elites view must be heard. We have some kind of State socialism in forestry in our country, which has to effectively filter through a democratic process. Under production forestry, private initiative needs encouragement through farm forestry and commercial forestry.

Forests and Tribals

There exists an age-old bond between the forest and tribal economies. Over time, the traditional rights of tribals on forests have shrunk. Shifting cultivation remains a sore area of conflict between the tribals and non-tribals. One latest estimate suggests that in Koraput, Kalahandi, Phulbani, Ganjam, Sambalpur, Sundargarh and Dhenkanal districts 1.41 lakh tribal families resort to this practice.[17] Around 7 to 10 lakh ha. of forest area is jhummed annually.[27] The area affected in the process is about 31 lakh ha. which is as high as 55 per cent of the recorded forests.[17] The role of Forest Department is crucial in any programme of tribal development. Tribal agriculture can be combined with forest development/Sloping Agricultural Land Technology (SALT) is such a strategy which can be introduced in the tribal economy[35, 36] by formulating separate physical micro plans for each hill/mountain based on the estimation of carrying capacity. Sustainability warrants estimation of population ceiling as shifting agriculture is clearly understood to be a sustainable system, provided that the land base is large enough in relation to population.[37]

Yield

The forest enrich the economy of Orissa with a large variety of products, a list of which would perhaps include several thousand diverse items[31] But the Forest Department keeps record of those which provide revenue classifying timber, firewood and bamboo as major and the rest as minor forest products. A comparison of the quinquennial average outturns of early 1960s with late 1980s shows that output of all products have fallen except kendu leaf, seeds, myrobalans and sabaigrass (Table 3.7). There is no recorded production of Kochila seeds, Pippal root, Chain climber, Nageswar flower, Bhuinimba, Petmuri fibre, Arjun bark, Kanta bandhuri, Katha lai and Bena chera. Fall in the output of many including the major products and non-availability of several items not only indicate loss of forests but also provide an index of deterioration of material welfare in Orissa.

So far as the contribution to the budgetary resources is concerned, Table 3.8 shows that over the four decades from 1951-52, the forests have generated a net non-tax revenue surplus of about Rs. 534 crores. The quinquennial growth indices record an exponential rise of about 65 times for revenue and 51 times for net surplus. Expenditure remained below 40 per cent of forest revenue until the last quinquennium, when the figure jumped to 48 per cent. Non-plan (normal) expenditure, mainly on forest administration claimed a large share until the first-half of the 1980s. It is only during 1986-91, the share of development in total expenditure on forests increased to a little above 62 per cent. The revenue growth rate of the 1970s could not be sustained through the 1980s. The rise and fall in revenue from timber and firewood in Table 3.9 suggest that the 1970s was the decade of large scale over-exploitation of forests.

TABLE 3.7 : Averag: Outturn of Forest Produce for the Quinquennium ending 1965-66 and 1988-89

(*Cum = Cubic metre and t = tonne*)

Sl. No.	*Name of the produce*	*Unit of measurement*	*Average of 1961-66*	*Average of 1984-89*	*Difference (Col. 5- Col. 4)*	*% of change*
1	*2*	*3*	*4*	*5*	*6*	*7*
Major Forest Products :						
1.	Timber	cum.× 10^5	5.6	2.3	– 3.3	41
2.	Firewood	cum. × 10^5	9.5	4.8	– 4.7	51
3.	Bamboo	t × 10^5	4.5[a]	2.7	– 1.8	60
Minor Forest Products :						
4.	Kendu leaves	t × 10^3	34.1	39.6	+ 5.5	116
5.	Sal Seeds	t × 10^3	20.2[b]	42.4	+ 22.2	210
6.	Vegetable and oil seeds	t × 10^3	3.1	48.9	+ 45.8	1577
7.	Drugs	t × 10^3	33.7	72.5	+ 38.8	215
8.	Tanstuff and Dye Stuff	t × 10^3	3.8	2.9	– 0.9	76
9.	Myrobolans	t × 10^3	1.8[c]	2.3	+ 0.5	128
10.	Gums and Resins	t × 10^3	0.7	0.4	– 0.3	57
11.	Fibre and flosses	t × 10^3	23.9	1.3	– 22.6	5
12.	Sabaigrass	t × 10^3	0.4[c]	0.4	—	—
13.	Honey and Wax	t × 10^2	7.8	0.5	– 7.3	6
14.	Lac	t × 10^2	1.1	0.6	– 0.5	55

Note : a 33 number of bamboos is equivalent to one tonne (14).
b Average of the quinquennium ending 1975-76.
c Average of the triennium ending 1979-80.

Source : 12, 13, 14 and 17.

In the forest product-mix of Orissa, kendu leaf is the highest revenue yielder. The product contributes more than 70 per cent of forest revenue. Its revenue was 2.8 times the total revenue earned from the three major products. Sal seed is another product, in the collection and processing of which ours is a pioneering State. As many as 10 medium-and small-scale solvent extraction industries have come up since 1972 to produce edible and non-edible oil from Sal seed and other minor seeds. In terms of revenue, rural and tribal employment, and industrial potential,

TABLE 3.8 : Quinquennial forest revenue and expenditure in Orissa, 1951-91

(Rs. × 10^7)

Sl. No.	Period	Total revenue		Total expenditure		Development (plan) expenditure		Net Surplus		Col. 5 as % of col. 3	Col. 7 as % of col. 3	Col. 7 as % of col. 5
		Amount	Index	Amount	Index	Amount	Index	Amount (Cols. 3-5)	Index			
1	2	3	4	5	6	7	8	9	10	11	12	13
1.	1951-56	5.98	100	2.01	100	0.17	100	3.97	100	33.6	2.8	8.5
2.	1956-61	12.97	217	3.95	197	0.49	288	9.02	227	30.5	3.8	12.4
3.	1961-66	20.17	337	7.75	386	2.59	1524	12.42	313	38.4	12.8	33.4
4.	1966-71	29.02	485	10.82	538	3.55	2088	18.20	458	37.3	12.2	32.8
5.	1971-76	46.57	779	17.75	883	4.70	2765	28.82	726	38.1	10.1	26.5
6.	1976-81	123.66	2068	40.42	2011	15.75	9265	83.24	2097	32.7	12.7	39.0
7.	1981-86	247.50	4139	71.99	3582	29.73	17488	175.51	4421	29.1	12.0	41.3
8.	1986-91	390.75	6534	188.32	9369	117.56	69153	202.43	5099	48.2	30.1	62.4
	Total	876.62	—	343.01	—	174.54	—	533.61	—	39.1	19.9	50.9

Source : 12, 13, 14, 15, 16 and 17.

TABLE 3.9 : Changing Structure of Forest Revenue in Orissa, 1961-91

(*Rs.* × 10^7)

Sl. No.	*Forest Produce/Share*	*1961-62*	*1971-72*	*1981-82*	*1990-91*
1	*2*	*3*	*4*	*5*	*6*
1.	Timber	1.81 (100)	2.98 (165)	25.41 (1404)	16.63 (919)
2.	Firewood	0.38 (100)	0.52 (137)	5.11 (1345)	4.46 (1174)
3.	Bamboo	0.21 (100)	0.56 (267)	3.84 (1829)	6.32 (3010)
4.	Kendu leaf	0.38 (100)	3.14 (826)	9.00 (2368)	76.85 (20224)
5.	Other minor forest produce	0.20 (100)	0.44 (220)	1.83 (915)	2.03 (1015)
6.	Miscellaneous	0.12 (100)	0.27 (225)	1.44 (1200)	2.76 (2300)
7.	Total	3.10 (100)	7.91 (255)	46.63 (1504)	109.05 (3518)
8.	Share of forest revenue in total State revenue (%)	8.3	5.2	7.8	4.4
9.	Share of forest in State non-tax revenue (%)	15.3	10.0	18.3	10.3
10.	Share of forest revenue in the State's own non-tax revenue (excluding grants) (%)	27.3	22.8	50.1	38.8

Note : Figures in the parentheses indicate growth indices. Growth indices with 1961-62 = 100.

Source : 12, 13, 14, 15, 16 and 17.

Kendu leaf and Sal seed appear to be the future major forest products of Orissa. The organisational basis for systematic collection of these needs to be strengthened.

Beyond This

Our exercise in forest policy and management impels us to spell out certain elements which should find articulation in policy declaration, objectives, underlying philosophical underpinnings and/or as essential action components.

1. Humankind's terrestrial home is threatened with impending environment disaster. To ward it off concern should dawn at

every level. That we are anxious to preserve and enhance the life support system of the mother earth has to find place.

2. The needs of animals along with the needs of human beings must now go into our economic calculus. Grassland, open space, scrub jungles should form a part of the forest system.
3. Human-nature relationship is intimate which has undergone successive changes. Human against nature approach needs reversal. Human in and with nature should ring through policy statements.
4. Thus far forests have been used as a natural resource. It has been an input in the development. We have to go further to see that extent and intensity of forest is an indicator of social progress and a component of net social welfare.
5. There has been great hiatus between policy, programmes and actions. Content analysis of newspaper reports corroborate this. This fervour with which Konark Hotel Complex has been piloted by the State government in utter disregard to environmental conditions and physical landscape for illusory material prosperity does not fit into the welfare concept (*The Prajatantra Saptahiki,* Vol. 1, No. 35, November 28-December 4, 1993 and *The Samaja*, 3-1-1994). Destruction of forests through nexus of local goons, forest contractors and officers is a daily occurrence (*The Sambad*, 31-12-1993). This, we are confident, is known to every body from the top to bottom. The destruction of mangrove forests in Bhitarakanika illustrates a kind of indifference on the part of the government which sends shivers down the spine (*The Prajatantra*, 23-10-1993, 23-11-1993 and 19 December 1993). When shall we heed these warnings?

NOTES

1. Anderson, T. and Bojo, J., 1992. The Economic Value of Forests, in A. Agarwal (Editor), *The Price of Forests, Centre for Science and Environment*, New Delhi, pp. 33-42.
2. Boulding, K.E., 1966. The Economics of the Coming Spaceship Earth, in H. Jarrett (Editor), *Environmental Quality in a Growing Economy : Resources for the Future*, The Johns Hopkins Press, Baltimore, pp. 3-14.
3. Chowdhry, K., 1992. Government Policies: Structural Changes for Better, in N. Ravi (Editor), *The Hindu Survey of the Environment*, 1992, M/S. Kasturi and Sons Ltd., Madras, pp. 31-33.

4. Das, S.S., 1992. *The State of Forests*, in *Orissa in Debate and Issues in Social Forestry in Orissa, Centre for Development Research and Training (CENDERET)*, Bhubaneswar, SIDA, New Delhi and ISO/Swedforest, Bhubaneswar, pp. 10-36.
5. Gadgil, M. and Guha, R., 1992. *New Forestry Policy: For Genuine Friendship*, in N. Ravi (Editor), *op. cit.*, pp. 26-29.
6. Government of India, 1976. *Report of the National Commission on Agriculture*, Part IX, Forestry, Ministry of Agriculture and Irrigation, New Delhi, pp. 457.
7. Government of India, 1980. *The Forest (Conservation) Act No. 69, Gazette of India, Extraordinary Part II, Sec. I*, 27th December, 1980.
8. Government of India, 1988. *The Forest (Conservation) Amendment Act No. 69, Gazette of India, Extraordinary Part II, Sec. I*, 17th December 1988.
9. Government of India, 1988. *National Forest Policy*. Ministry of Environment and Forests, New Delhi.
10. Government of Orissa, 1959. *Report of the Forest Enquiry Committee*, Development Department, Bhubaneswar, pp. 212.
11. Government of Orissa, 1961. *Forests of Orissa*. Forest Department, Cuttack, pp. 43.
12. Government of Orissa, 1968. *Hand-Book of Forest Statistics*, Office of the Chief Conservator of Forests (CCF), pp. 77.
13. Government of Orissa, 1974. *Handbook of Forest Statistics*, CCF, pp. 91.
14. Government of Orissa, 1983. *The Statistical Outline of Orissa Forest*, CCF, pp. 170.
15. Government of Orissa, 1990. *Orissa Forests* (Brochure), Principal CCF, Bhubaneswar.
16. Government of Orissa, 1990. *Orissa Budget in Brief, 1990-91*. Directorate of Economics & Statistics (DES), Bhubaneswar, pp. 58.
17. Government of Orissa, 1991. *A Decade of Forestry in Orissa: 1981-1990*. Principal CCF, Mimeo.
18. Government of Orissa, 1991. *Estimates of State Domestic Product: 1950-51 to 1988-89*, DES, Bhubaneswar, pp. 164.
19. Kant, S., Singh, N.M. and Singh, K.K. 1991. *Community Based Forest Management Systems (Case Studies from Orissa)*, Indian Institute of Forest Management, Bhopal; SIDA, New Delhi and ISO/Swedforest, New Delhi. pp. 70.
20. Meadows, D.H., Meadows, D.L., Randers, J. and Behrens III, W.W., 1972. *The Limits to Growth: A Report for the Club of Rome's Project on Predicament of Mankind*, Universe Books, New York.
21. Mishan, E.J., 1967. *The Costs of Economic Growth*, Staples Press, Pelican edition, 1969, pp. 240.
22. Mishan, E.J., 1973. Growth and Antigrowth: What are the Issues in A. Weintraub, E. Schwartz and J. Aronson (Editors), *The Economic Growth Controversy*, Macmillan, London, pp. 3-38.
23. Nayak, B. and Sahu, N.C., 1993. Economic-ecologic Value of Forestry in Orissa, in S.N. Misra (Editor), *Orissa Economy: Problems and Prospects* (Accepted), in press.
24. Padhi, G.S., 1991. *Forest Resources of Orissa*. Dr. S.S. Padhi, Arunalaya, Bhubaneswar, Third Revised and Enlarged Edition, pp. 343.
25. Pant, M.M. 1977. *Forestry Sector: Its Contribution to Gross National Product*, Indian Forester, Vol. 103, No. 11, pp. 739-769.
26. Patnaik, L.K., Egneus, H. and Das, S.S., 1989. *Social Forestry Handbook for Orissa*, Vol. I. SIDA and ISO/Swedforest, Bhubaneswar, pp. 108.

27. Patnaik, N., 1993. *Swidden Cultivation Amongst Two Tribes of Orissa. Cenderet*, SIDA and ISO/Swedforest, Bhubaneswar, pp. 99.
28. Pearce, D., 1991. *An Economic Approach to Saving the Tropical Forests*, in D. Helm (Editor), *Economic Policy Towards the Environment*, Basil Blackwell, Oxford, pp. 240-262.
29. Sahu, N.C., and Das, B., 1979. *An Appraisal of Forest Policy in Orissa, Indian Forester*, Dehra Dun, Vol. 105, No. 1, pp. 41-49.
30. Sahu, N.C., and Das, B., 1983. *Forest Policy of Orissa, Proceedings of Environmental Education Curricula*, and *Environment and Natural Resources Management*, Orissa Environmental Society, Bhubaneswar, 4-5 June 1983, pp. 124-133.
31. Sahu, N.C., 1986. *Economics of Forest Resources: Problems and Policies in a Regional Economy*, B.R. Publishing Corporation, Delhi, pp. 360.
32. Sahu, N.C., and Nayak, B., 1993. *Niche diversification in Environmental/ ecological Economics, Ecological Economics*, Elsevier, Amsterdam (Accepted), in Press.
33. Schumachar, E.F., 1968. *Buddhist Economics*, in H.E. Daly (Editor), Toward a Steady-State Economy, W.H. Freeman and Company, San Francisco, pp. 231-239.
34. Schumachar, E.F., 1973. *Small is Beautiful: Economics as if People Mattered*, Harper Torch Books, London.
35. SIDA, CENDERET, ISO/Swedforest, 1990. *Helping Forest Dwellers of Orissa to Adopt Viable Alternatives to Shifting Cultivation*, Bhubaneswar, pp. 104.
36. SIDA, CENDERET, ISO/Swedforest, 1992. *Sloping Agricultural Land Technology (SALT): An Alternative to Shifting Cultivation in Orissa*, Bhubaneswar, pp. 112.
37. World Bank, 1991. *The Forest Sector: A World Bank Policy Paper*, Washington, D.C. pp. 98.
38. World Bank, 1992. Development and Environment, *World Development Report 1992*, Oxford University Press, New York, pp. 308.

4

TOWARDS A NEW FOREST POLICY

— Nimai Bhai

History and Background

In Resolution No. 13/52-F dated the 12th May 1952, the Government of India in the erstwhile Ministry of Food and Agriculture enunciated a Forest Policy to be followed in the management of State Forests in the country. However over the years, forests in the country have suffered serious depletion. This is attributable to relentless pressures arising from ever-increasing demand for fuel-wood fodder and timber, inadequacy of protection measures, diversion of forest lands for non-forest uses without ensuring compensatory afforestation and essential environmental safeguards and the tendency to look upon forests as revenue earning resource. The need is to review the situation and to evolve for future, a new strategy of forest conservation and improvement of natural environment. With this preamble, the Government of India in the Ministry of Environment and Forests passed another Resolution dated 7th December 1988 which is known as National Forest Policy, 1988.

National Forest Policy

The basic objectives that should govern the National Forest Policy are as follows:

- Maintenance of environmental stability through preservation, and where necessary, restoration of the ecological balance that has been adversely disturbed by serious depletion of the forests of the country.
- Conserving the natural heritage of the country by preserving the remaining natural forests with the vast varieties of flora and

fauna, which represent the remarkable biological diversity and resources of the country.

— Checking soil erosion and denundation in the catchment areas of rivers, lakes, reservoirs in the interest of soil and water conservation, for mitigating floods and droughts and for the retardation of siltation of reservoirs.
— Checking the extension of sand-dunes in the desert areas in Rajasthan and along the coast tracts.
— Increasing substantially the forest/tree cover in the country through massive afforestation and social forestry programmes especially on all denuded, degraded and improductive lands.
— Meeting the requirements of fuelwood, fodder, minor forest produces and small timber of the rural and tribal populations.
— Increasing the productivity of forests to meet essential needs.
— Encouraging efficient utilisation of forest produce and maximising substitution of wood.
— Creating a massive people's movement with the involvement of women, for achieving these objectives and to minimise pressure on existing forests.

The principal aim of Forest Policy must be to ensure environmental stability and maintenance of ecological balance including atmospheric equilibrium which are vital for subsistence of all lifeforms, human, animal, birds and plants. The derivation of direct economic benefit must be subordinated to this principal aim.

Keeping this preamble and basic objectives in view essentials of forest management, strategy, management of State Forests, Rights and concessions, wildlife conservation, Tribal people and Forests, shifting cultivation, damage to forests from encroachments, fires and grazing, forest based industries, forest extension, forest education, forestry research, forest survey and data base, legal support and infrastructure development and financial support for forestry policies were framed on the basis of which "The Forest (Conservation) Amendment Act 1988 (No. 69 of 1988)" was promulgated to amend the Forest (Conservation) Act, 1980.

Reactions and Actions

This amended Act had a country-wide reactions among the tribals at large; the tribal leaders, Tribal Members of the Parliament, Non-Governmental Voluntary Organisations and Social activists who are closely linked at grass-root level working with the forest dwellers and tribals in different States. The Act did not give any privileges or rights to the forest-dwellers mostly the tribals who live on forests and whose survival solely depend on forests.

People's 'Representatives' Reaction and the Prime Minister

A large number of delegates who attended the National Conference on Panchayat Raj and Scheduled Tribes held in March, 1989 expressed their resentment against the provisions of the amended Forest (Conservation) Act. They also pointed out that the Forest (Conservation) Act, 1980 and the declared National Forest Policy, 1988 are contradictory to each other. They, therefore made a strong plea for suitable amendments of the Forest (Conservation) Act, so as to mitigate the hardship faced by them like :

(a) Large extent of forest land which is under the possession and cultivation of tribals is not regularised by conferring ownership rights upon them.

(b) Tribal dwellers of forest villages who depend on the forest are deprived of developmental activities because developmental activities and projects cannot be taken up in these areas due to various restrictions imposed by Forest (Conservation) Act. It was also stated by one and all that small projects like construction of irrigation tanks and wells, school buildings, dispensaries, drinking water wells, *Nistar* tanks, etc. could not be taken up in tribal areas due to these restrictions.

(c) The delegates also complained that due to the provisions of Forest (Conservation) Act, the grazing of their cattle is restricted. They are not able to procure adequate supply of fodder, minor timber, fuel wood etc. for their day to day requirements.

Shri Rajiv Gandhi, the then Prime Minister, reacting to the tribal's sentiments stated that he felt deeply concerned about certain undesirable things that have happened. He declared that the forest policy with regard to the tribals needed to be reviewed.

Efforts of NGO Sector

The NGO sector appointed a three men Committee who collected the views of forest-dwellers and tribals from different parts of the country and presented a memorandum to the Prime Minister, Forest Ministry and the President of India on this issue. The Memorandum represented the sentiments of forest-dwellers living in different parts of the country. A draft Forest Bill 1989 was also placed for the consideration of the Government of India. Government appointed a Committee under the Chairmanship of Shri Duleep Mathai to go into details of the issues and recommend to the Government for corrections in the existing Forest Laws. The National Commission For Scheduled Castes and Scheduled Tribes organised a National Workshop on 21st September 1989 at New Delhi where all the issues and problems of the Forest Laws were discussed in detail and Shri Duleep Mathai, Chairman of the Committee attended and participated in the discussions. The Mathai Committee placed its recommendations in time and finally instead of changing the National Policy and Forest Laws it amended some of the Sections and articles of the law to suit the sentiments of the forest dwellers mostly the tribals.

Feelings and Suggestions

But I feel that unless the Government re-think the issues afresh and declare a new National Forest Policy and accept the basic rights and need of the forest-dwellers and tribals and change the law accordingly the problem will not be solved. Hence it is time to make the Government understand the different issues and problems created out of its policy and the amended Act.

The National Forest Policy, 1988 aims to preserve existing forest wealth; help the Government to increase its income by commercial utilisation, to maintain the ecological and environmental balance of the country at large. It has overlooked the interests of the poor forest dwellers mostly the tribals and backward people who live on it. The Policy clearly indicates that the Government owns all the forests throughout the country. The new policy should be, like landownership, the forests should be owned by the forest dwellers and claim a nominal forest revenue like land revenue. This may be done after proper survey of all actual forest lands available in the country.

(2) Only reserve forests which are now under actual tree cover may be owned by the Government and all other varieties of land in the forest-land record may be assigned to the forest-dwellers considering the individual community needs to individuals and the village community.

(3) The present joint-management system (by village committees) may be withdrawn and like revenue lands, forest lands may be settled.

(4) Forest management system which is now under different categories like working plan, plantation, social forestry, territorial, bamboo, tendu leaves etc. may be consolidated into one. The area of forest zones may be small and consolidated. All the process of forest management through conservation, vegetation, protection, exploitation and commercial utilisation of timber, forest products, fuel wood etc. may vest with the small groups of forest officials and employees for its able management.

(5) Finances may be allotted according to the needs of that area after a proper planning and achievements of the area and a target may be fixed accordingly keeping in mind the environment and ecological balances of that area.

(6) Specific responsibilities with division of work may be fixed for individual employees and officials of the Forest Department for each zone.

(7) The management of State forests may be done on the lines as mentioned above.

Separate village schools may be started to educate the villagers and local foresters.

The new Forest Policy may have such clear indications and directives to give it a national shape.

5

FOREST POLICY AND TRIBAL DEVELOPMENT

— Jagannath Shroff

Tribals constitute the bulk of the population living below the poverty line. The economic development of the district is inextricably connected with the upliftment of the tribals. Apart from the fact that forests provided the main source for food, shelter and to some extent clothing, the tribal communities have had a symbiotic relationship with the forests. The customs of tribal life including religious and social functions and folklore have been shaped and formed by forests. In times of distress and scarcity tribals mostly rely on forest produce for their subsistence and in normal times their food comprises tuber, roots, fruits and leaves collected from forests. Thus tribal life is connected in one way or other, intimately with the forests. They have lived in perfect harmony with forests for generations and their culture has revolved round this life-style. As of right, they cultivate forest lands and collect minor forest produce to eke out their livelihood because they are the original inhabitants of forest areas. The privileges enjoyed by the tribals are regulated by the forest policy of the State. But unfortunately this policy was not operated in a manner which can convince the tribals that protection and reservation of forests was in their interest. On the other hand the tribals who considered themselves to be the owners of all the forests, have come to feel that they have been deprived of their own habitat. The crux of the problem is to create a nexus between forest development and tribal economy by taking full advantage of the tremendous attachment of the tribals to the forests and utilising the same for intensive development of forest growth and tribal advancement.

Man's attempt at the intensification of the use of natural resources can often result in the exhaustion of the resources or deterioration in other interacting resources. More intensive utilization of the natural resources of earth has undermined all economic development. According to a tentative estimate about five lakh acres of lands (which comprised about one lakh acres of cultivated lands belonging to mostly tribals and about four lakhs acres of forest lands including submersible areas of reservoirs) have been utilised for the execution of several major development projects. About two lakh acres of forest lands have been released to the Dandakaranya Development Authority alone after deforestation in Umerkote and Malkangiri Zones for resettlement purposes. Thus about one lakh tribals in all have been deprived of about five lakh acres of private and forest lands on which they depended for their livelihood. Those dispossessed from their own habitats account for more than twenty thousand. The compensation paid for acquisition of private lands under the Land Acquisition Act was very nominal. Not all the displaced persons have been properly resettled by providing alternative lands and common amenities. Particularly due to construction of the Chitrakonda Reservoir twenty thousand tribal people living in 151 villages covering 316 Sq. Kms. adjoining Andhra Pradesh in Chitrakonda Tehsil and Kudumulugumma Block remain isolated from the rest of the District. Same is the case in respect of the group of villages lying on the other side of Jalaput Dam. No development work worth the name has been taken up in this vast area which remains cut off due to lack of regular communication facilities. There is growing discontentment and frustration amongst the people of the area, which remains unapproachable. For no fault of theirs and due to irony of fate that instead of reaping the fruits of development, these people are the victims of ill-conceived planning. This is a glaring instance of the worst effect of the major development projects, on tribal life in the region.

The Constitutional provisions, particularly those relating to protection of economic interests of tribals and safeguarding their way of life was expected to have far reaching effect to ensure their development and taking their right place in the general life of the country. But the desired results still remain unachieved for obvious reasons. Paradoxically the process of tribal development had created contradictory conditions in their cultural development . While on the one hand due to the impact of development, the tribals are uprooted from their cultural moorings, on the other hand it indirectly reinforced their cultural identities.

Development is a process directed at achieving the desired state of material and social well-being through the optimum utilisation of capital, labour and natural resources. But how best development process can be used as an effective tool to achieve the goal of economic development is the task that planners and implementing agencies would have to carefully consider.

Forests play a major role in regulating socio-economic condition of a country besides controlling the ecological balance. Over the years forests in the country have suffered serious depletion. This is attributable to relentless pressures arising from ever increasing demand for fuelwood and timber due to explosive population growth diversion of forest lands for non-forest uses, indiscriminate cutting of trees and the tendency to look upon forests as revenue earning source. Forest conservation has now become quite imperative and to meet this challenge the Government of India were pleased to formulate and issue the National Forest Policy on 7th December 1988. Amongst other things it emphasises the need for maintenance of environmental stability through preservation and restoration of ecological balance, increasing substantially the forest/tree cover through massive afforestation and social forestry programmes to meet the requirement of fuelwood, fodder, minor forest produce and small timber of the rural and tribal population. Much stress has been laid on the essentials of forest management, strategy, rights and concessions, strict regulation of diversion of forest lands for non-forest purpose, close association of tribal people in the development of forests in view of the symbiotic relationship which they have with forests, etc. Unfortunately, the State government have not yet revised their earlier policy to tackle the present day problems effectively. It is high time that the policy of the State government should be formulated without further delay for the management, preservation and development of forests.

Under the changed circumstances plantation has assumed importance in the present day planning and utilisation of Government wastelands. Guidelines for selection of lands for various plantation schemes were issued by Government in Forest, Fisheries and Animal Husbandry Department Memo No. 20432/FFAH dated 14th July, 1977. But the results of the study undertaken by Orissa Drought Action Forum Advocacy Cell through the Council of Professional Social Workers, Bhubaneswar in some parts of Koraput region, indicate that concerted efforts towards afforestation by government agencies and other private agencies (Industrial houses) were only directed towards commercial plantations, particularly eucalyptus which is considered to have adverse effects on the soil and ecosystem. This indeed is a matter of great concern as it is contrary to the guidelines issued in the past and the necessity of social and mixed forestry has been overlooked. Proper selection of sites has not been done by the different agencies executing these schemes. Dongor lands under the occupation of tribals for long have been brought under such schemes, depriving them of the benefit of using these lands. Thus they have been displaced and dispossessed resulting in a lot of discontentment.

It may also be relevant to point out that Dr. Neelakanth Rath, Ex-Director of Gokhale Institute of Politics and Economics and at present in the Indian School of Political Economy, Pune and Member, Planning Board, Orissa in his note on 'Approach to Tribal Area Development' which was presented in the seminar organised by C.O.A.T.S. on 7th January, 1994 at Koraput, while stressing the need for afforestation schemes, observed that the work of afforestation in Kashipur project is not being executed by the village Panchayat with the cooperation of the villagers. He, therefore, emphasised the necessity of directly associating the villagers in the execution of the project. He clearly explained the difference between handing over public land to the village people for social forestry and the social forestry work undertaken by government. He was of the view that if the area had been clearly marked out and initially allotted to the villagers individually, and then the village panchayat had been entrusted with the execution of the work under the informal advice of the State officers, it would have been reasonable to expect proper motivation and sense of belonging. This is in response to the observations made by the Development Commissioner and Additional Chief Secretary to the Government in his inspection notes of the project dated 2nd March 1993 to the effect that the local officers were bemoaning as the beneficiaries were mainly interested in demanding wages, the output was very poor and the sense of belonging and motivation was practically non-existent. This again is an instance of execution of the scheme disregarding the approved guidelines.

The word 'Forest' has not been defined either in the Orissa Forest Act or the Forest Conservation Act. It is merely used in its widest significance. At the instance of some industrial houses like Mangalam Timbers, Sewa Papers etc. agriculture lands are used for raising commercial plantations. In the absence of a clear definition of the term 'Forest' doubt arises whether such commercial plantations can be treated as forests as they cannot be brought under the purview of 'Agriculture' as defined in Section 2 of the O.L.R. Act. Thus it amounts to putting agricultural land to non-agricultural use attracting the provision of Section 8 of the O.L.R. Act. Moreover, if they are treated as 'Forest Lands' because of their utilisation to raise plantation, they attract the provisions of Section 2 of the Forest Conservation Act in the event of using them again for agricultural purposes. This gives rise to an anamolous position. The legal implications have to be made clear.

Waste lands of government are notified for reservation under Section 4(1) of the Orissa Forest Act. Proposals for reservation of Forest Blocks include reserved lands, protected lands and unserved lands. While reserved and protected lands are identifiable in the cadastral maps, the unreserved lands are not borne out in any of the village maps as they have been left out of village areas unsurveyed in some portions of Koraput District, particularly in Gunupur, Pottangi, Machkund, Bissamcuttack, Koraput Tehsil areas, during last survey. Fresh survey has to be undertaken to identify them properly and in the meantime all such lands have also been encroached upon. In the absence of mention of plot numbers in respect of these unsurveyed lands in the reservation proposals it becomes difficult to distinguish the Government and private lands.

To sum up, a clear-cut forest policy of the State government has to be formulated in consonance with the National Forest Policy of 1988, taking the various aspects into consideration in view of the discussions in the foregoing paragraphs. Legislative changes are necessary in the Forest and Revenue laws to avoid conflict and proper implementation of different afforestation schemes on both government and private lands, as this has a great bearing on the economic development of the tribals. The need for social forestry and mixed forests is more for the benefit of the tribals, than commercial plantations which mainly help industries. Efforts are also called for to increase the production of minor forest produce including medicinal plants by bringing more areas under such plantation. More and more numbers of cottage and small scale industries are to be set up to process the minor forest produce as finished products will fetch more price than raw produce in the market and at the same time it will create opportunities for gainful employment. The Forest policy of the State should take into account all such vital matters in the interests of economic development of tribals.

6

FOREST POLICY AND TRIBAL DEPRIVATION

— *P.C. Mohapatro*

An official policy statement is made to meet the needs in the country as a whole. When there are conflicting interests by different classes of people, the policy statement tries to cater to the needs of all the classes. However, in a democratic country like ours, the interest of the powerful classes always takes over the interest of the powerless or weaker classes of society.

A study of the history of the National Forest Policy lucidly brings out the compromises made from time to time to strike a balance between the conflicting interests. Initially the need for expansion of agriculture gained precedence over others. Gradually when the industrial development of the country gained momentum, Forest Policies were oriented to meet the raw-material requirement for the forest based industries. With the fast depletion of forests when the ecological conditions deteriorated at a rapid rate, maintenance of ecological equilibrium was given priority over other needs. However, over the years the various forest policies enunciated from time to time have always tried to restrict the rights and privileges of the tribals who are mainly forest dwellers and dependent on forests in a variety of ways. They have always been looked upon as unwarranted intruders and destroyers of forests. Forest policies have been often viewed as anti-people and anti-tribal policies. Hence, it is necessary to briefly discuss the Forest Policies enunciated from time to time in our country.

Development of Indian Forest Policy and Legislation

Before the advent of British, there was only a regulation by custom of the people's rights over forests and forest produce. However, the availability of vast tracts of forest and small population did not create any problem. Forest based industries were practically non-existent. Custom and religious faith prohibited cutting of certain trees like the *banyan*, the *peepal* and the fruit bearing trees. Beyond this, the forest dwellers had complete freedom to exploit forest wealth.

It was only on August 3, 1855 that the British rulers issued a memorandum regulating the movement of forest dwellers in forests. This was replaced by the Forest Act of 1865 which empowered the Government to declare any land covered with trees, jungle as Government forest by notification, provided such notification should not abridge or effect any existing rights of individuals or communities. The increasing realisation of commercial value of the forests by the British, made them amend the Forest Legislations in 1878 which further limited the rights of the forest dwellers. (D'Abreo, 1982).

The first official forest policy of the Government of India was pronounced in 1894. It was based on Voelcker's report on 'improvement of Indian Agriculture'. It aimed at maintenance of adequate forest for the preservation of climatic and physical conditions of the country. In order to attain this objective it emphasised on the regulation of rights and restriction of privileges, previously enjoyed by the inhabitants of immediate neighbourhood. (G.S. Chandra, 1970). Dr. Voelcker discussed the role of forests vis-a-vis agriculture and stressed the need for formulating a forest policy with a definite bias for serving agricultural interests more directly than before (K.P. Sagreiya, 1967). This statement of the Forest policy of India became the basis for drawing the forest policies of various countries of the erstwhile British empire. The basic principles laid down in this policy documents were:

(i) The sole object with which State forests are administered is public benefit and therefore *preservation of forest involve the regulation of rights and restriction of privileges of the user of the forest by the neighbouring population.*

(ii) Forest situated on the hill slopes should be maintained as protected forests to preserve the climatic and physical conditions of the country, and to protect the cultivated plains that lie below them from the devastating action of hill torrents.

(iii) Forests which are the store house of valuable timbers should be managed on *commercial lines as a source of revenue to the State.*

(iv) If a demand for agriculture land arises and can be met from forest alone, it should be conceded without hesitation, provided honeycombing of valuable forests should be discouraged and permanent cultivation encouraged within limits.

(v) Forests that yield only inferior timber, fuelwood or fodder or used for grazing, should be managed mainly in the interest of local population, care being taken to see that the user does not annihilate its subject and the people are protected against their own improvidence.

Thus the policy emphasised the commercial use of forests as also its ecological value. It paved the way for the regulation of rights and privileges of forest dwellers over forest land and produce. What is more important to note here is that no study was made of the requirements of forest dwellers before earmarking village forests. Often forests set aside for the villagers were far below the area required by the inhabitants (Sarad Kulkarni, 1983).

After independence, it was considered necessary to revise the Indian Forest Policy. The new policy stated that the value of forests was recognised not only in physical field, such as conservation of moisture and prevention of erosion, but also in the economic field such as development of agriculture, industry and communication. Accordingly the Revised Forest Policy of 1952 was based on the 'Paramounts needs' of the country and emphasised the need for evolving a balanced and complementary land-use. It classified forest on a functional basis i.e., protected Forests, National Forests, Village Forests and Tree lands. The re-orientation of forest policy further curtailed the rights of tribals on forests. The new policy came into operation with a statement which clarified the local needs as follows:

"Village communities in the neighbourhood of forest will naturally make greater use of its products for satisfaction of their domestic and agricultural needs. Such use, however, in no event be permitted at a cost of national interests. The accident of a village being close to a forest does not prejudice the rights of a country as a whole to receive the benefit of a national asset. The scientific conservation of a forest inevitably involved the regulation of rights and restriction of privileges of user depending upon the value and importance of the forest, however, irksome such restraint may be to the neighbouring areas".

A study of the new forest policy would indicate that the following changes were made which were of great concern to the tribals:

(1) It withdrew the concessions to release forest land for cultivation;

(2) It restricted the use of the outlying areas in the reserved forests to meet the villagers' need and decided that there should be village forest for the purpose;
(3) It brought under control free grazing of forests and free enjoyment of private forests; and
(4) It aimed at discouraging tribals to do away from the practice of shifting cultivation through persuasion.

This policy interpreted the concept of national interest in a very narrow sense. The destruction of forests for construction of roads, buildings of irrigation and hydro-electric projects etc. was justified in the name of 'national interest' whereas cultivation of lands classed as forest lands but without any actual tree cover was treated as encroachment. (Sharad Kulkarni, 1983). Moreover, a clear new emphasis was given to the commercial utilisation of forests in this policy (D'Abreo, 1982). Further, the policy recognised a basic contradiction between the national interest and the interest of the forest dwellers. A major lacuna in the Forest Policy was its failure to spell out the alternatives that were being offered where the rights of tribals were to be abridged or cancelled in the larger public interest (Chandrasekharan, 1983).

The Central Board of Forestry and the Estimate Committee of the Lok Sabha in the 76th report recommended a reappraisal of the National Forest Policy of 1952 and introduction of suitable agri-silvicultural measures for the benefit of the tribals and provision of alternative means of livelihood to wean them away from shifting cultivation. (Mohapatro, P.C. *et al.*, 1984). It has been pointed out by Dhebar Commission that forests are to be used as agencies of economic uplift of tribals and not as instrument of harassment.

The National Commission of Agriculture (N.C.A.) also suggested a revised forest policy taking into account two main issues: (a) meeting the needs of rural community, and (b) satisfying the needs of protective and recreative functions of forests. They suggested that the revised forest policy should indicate the inter-relationship of forest economy with rural and tribal economy and the factors to be considered are: (a) employment, (b) rights of users, and (c) involvement of local people. They have advocated that tribal welfare should be ensured by making arrangements to satisfy their domestic needs for various forest products and by reorganising their priority need of direct employment in forestry operation. However, "it does not touch such basic-questions as the future of traditional rights of the tribal communities in respect of forests and other resources and statutory provisions about a broad based participation in developmental planning, preparation of working plan and management of forests". (Roy Burman, B.K. 1980.)

This view is further strengthened by the observation made by M.K. Chakravarti, former Deputy Chief Conservator of Forests, Madhya Pradesh when he states that, "for over a century the forest department has been made to be quasi-commercial department, but never a quasi-social or quasi-welfare department. . . . The use and outside sale of fuel should be regulated subject to the availability of other sources of income to the villages". (Srikant, M.L., 1982.)

The National Forest Policy was reviewed and revised in 1988. In the preamble of the policy, the government has indicated the causes of serious depletion of forest in the country. They are: "relentless pressure arising from everincreasing demand for fuelwood, fodder and timber, inadequacy of protection measures, diversion of forest land to non-forest use without ensuring compensatory afforestation and essential environmental safeguards; and the tendency to look upon forests as revenue earning resource". (Government of India, 1988: 1.1.)

Like the 1952 document, the policy also states as its objectives, the maintenance of environmental stability, conserving the natural heritage, checking soil erosion, increasing the forest tree cover, meeting people's fuelwood, timber and minor forest produce requirements, encouraging efficient use of forest produce and creating massive people's movement around afforestation, (Government of India 1988: 2:1). These objectives are more or less the same as those of the 1952 policy, but they are spelt out much more clearly. Besides, the objective of ecological balance has been given priority over other objectives.

A strategy has been worked out in the policy statement itself to achieve the objectives. It has emphasised that a massive need-based and time bound tree planting programme should be undertaken on a priority basis on all degraded and denuded lands, for fuelwood and fodder development. At the same time, it is stated that the national needs should be taken care of. The emphasis is on the State controlling and plantation and afforestation programmes and the forest management in general. The policy makers have expressed their intention that all M.F.P. needs are to be met through State run depots (*ibid.*, 4.2 and 4.3).

The present policy has more people oriented statements and it has tried to remove many anti-people views of earlier policy statements. However, it still retains the concept exclusive State ownership of forests. It mentions industrial requirement as national needs and the requirements of tribals and other forest dwellers are people's needs. It is at this stage that the Forest Policy, 1988 seems to create a contradiction between national and people's needs. It emphasises that both of them should be subordinated to environmental stability. "Studies have shown that when all the needs are put together without a concrete strategy in favour of the poor, the implementation strengthens the powerful sectors that call themselves the protectors of national needs. (Walter Fernandes, 1992.)

It may be noted that environment does not only connote "beautiful trees and tigers", but also includes within its scope the people and specially those communities who have traditionally depended on forests for their livelihood. Thus control of these resources by the corporate sector for purposes of making profit has now deprived the tribals their mode of survival.

We can take for instance the cases of Orissa State and Koraput district. There is scarcity of accurate date on the extent of forest available. Even official data published from time to time by various departments do not tally with each other. An examination of Table 6.1 to Table 6.4, appended to this chapter will make this fact clear to us.

TABLE 6.1: Classification of Forest Area by Legal Status in Koraput District (Undivided)

(Area in Sq. Kms.)

Year	*No. of Forest Divisions*	*Area in Square Kilometres*				*Percentage of forest area to the total geographical area of the dist.*
		Reserved	*Protected*	*Others unclassed*	*Total*	
1	2	3	4	5	6	7
1969-70	03	5253.24	246.16	4854.98	10,354.38	38.40
1970-71	03	5253.24	246.16	4854.98	10,354.38	38.40
1971-72	03	2170.31	5,420.41	1058.71	8,649.43	32.07
1972-73	03	1566.93	599.38	4205.61	6,371.92	23.63
1973-74	03	2191.65	362.82	8871.53	11,426.30	42.36
1974-75	03	2191.65	369.03	8865.63	11,426.31	42.36
1975-76	03	48.57	4,035.32	3526.45	7,610.34	28.16
1976-77	03	156.80	3,986.47	4145.43	8,288.70	30.68
1977-78	03	201.58	2,788.40	9074.79	12,034.77	44.54
1978-79	03	445.76	2,631.99	9428.80	12,506.55	46.28
1979-80	03	602.68	11,416.58	0.55	12,019.81	44.96
1980-81	04	657.59	11,521.36	0.50	12.219.45	45.96
1981-82	04	697.59	11,521.36	0.50	12,219.45	45.96
1982-83	04	1792.49	6,928.09	0.49	8,721.07	32.35

(Contd.)

(*TABLE 6.1 contd.*)

1	2	3	4	5	6	7
1983-84	04	1929.21	6,914.59	0.52	8,844.32	32.80
1984-85	04	1964.38	6,964.25	0.52	8,929.15	33.12
1985-86	04	2146.40	5,102.12	0.84	7,249.36	26.89
1986-87	04	2138.97	5,934.00	739.44	8,812.41	32.68
1987-88	04	2144.16	5,928.71	793.91	8,866.78	32.89
1988-89	04	2144.16	5,928.71	793.91	8,866.78	32.89
1989-90	04	2144.16	5,947.93	774.49	8,866.58	32.89

Note : The percentage of forest area indicated in column 7 in respect of 1971-72 and 1972-73 is less as the information in respect of Jeypore forest Division has not been included in the district Statistical Hand Book due to non-receipt of the same by the D.S.O. Information 1981-82 onwards has been obtained from the Principal, Chief Conservator of Forests, Orissa, Bhubaneswar instead from D.F.O.'s by the D.S.O.

Source : 1. District Statistical Officer, Koraput: *District Statistical Hand Book, 1971*, O.G.P. 1974, pp. 226.

2. District Statistical Officer, Koraput: *Dist. Statistical Hand Book-1974 and 1975*, O.G.P. 1978, pp. 85-88.
3. *Dist. Statistical Hand Book, Koraput, 1976-77*, O.G.P. 1982, pp. 147-148.
4. *Dist. Statistical Hand Book, Koraput, 1978 and 1979*, O.G.P. 1983, p. 87.
5. *Dist. Statistical Hand Book, Koraput, 1980-1981*, O.G.P. 1987, p. 154.
6. *Dist. Statistical Hand Book, Koraput, 1989-90*, O.G.P. 1991, p. 55.
7. Directorate of Economics & Statistics, Orissa, Bhubaneswar: *Dist. Statistical Hand Book, Koraput, 1990-91*, O.G.P. 1992, p. 22.

Table 6.1 and 6.3 deals with classification of forest area by legal status in respect of undivided Koraput district and Orissa. During the period 1980-81 to 1989-90, the percentage of forest to the total geographical area has been reduced by 13.07 per cent and 3.10 per cent respectively in case of the district and the State. Similarly, Table 6.3 and 6.4 deals with classification of forests by land utilisation pattern in case of undivided Koraput district and Orissa State. During the same period, the percentage of forest to the total geographical area has reduced by 18.98 per cent and 7.80 per cent respectively in respect of the district and the State. It is evident from all available sources that the area of forest to the total geographical area is decreasing at a faster rate in case of Koraput district.

Construction of public projects alone in Koraput district has led to the destruction of forests to a tune of 98,427.85 hactares during the last 34 years period. In addition, the commercial exploitation of forest resources in the district during the period from 1983-84 to 1987-88 has given increasing rate of profit. An analysis of the forest revenue and forest expenditure as given in Table 6.5 clearly reveals the position.

TABLE 6.2(A) : Classification of Forest Area by Legal Status in Orissa

(Forest Area in Sq. Kms.)

Sl. No.	*Year*	*Area of the State*	*Reserved Forest*	*Protected Forest*	*Total area under Forest Deptt.*	*Proportion of forest to the whole area of the State*	*Remarks*
1	*2*	*3*	*4*	*5*	*6*	*7*	*8*
1.	1936-37	84,680	4,628.33	528.36	5,156.69	6.10	Figures given in sq. miles have been converted into sq. kms.
2.	1940-41	84,680	7,940.94	541.31	8,482.25	10.00	
3.	1945-46	84,680	6,254.85	639.73	6,894.58	8.10	
4.	1948-49	1,55,752	21,455.56	21,626.50	43,082.06	27.70	
5.	1950-51	1,55,752	22,975.89	22,740.20	45,716.09	29.40	
6.	1952-53	1,55,752	26,332.53	35,280.98	61,613.51	39.60	

Source : Govt. of Orissa, Bureau of Statistics and Economics, Finance Department, Statistical Abstracts of Orissa, Vol. 1-A, Goswami Press, Cuttack, 1957, p. 31.

TABLE 6.2(B) : Classification of Forest Area by Legal Status in Orissa

Sl. No.	*Year*	*Area in Square Kilometers*				*Percentage of the forest area to the total geographical area*	*Remarks*
		Reserved	*Protected*	*Others Unclassified*	*Total*		
1.	1952-53	25,398	18,122	—	43,520	27.9	
2.	1955-56	26,651	18,731	—	45,382	29.1	
3.	1960-61	22,492	43,359	—	65,851	42.3	
4.	1965-66	29,690	38,516	12	68,218	43.0	
5.	1970-71	23,874	43.881	13	67,768	43.6	
6.	1975-76	25.984	41,131	16	67,131	43.1	
7.	1980-81	24,987	34,961	15	59,963	38.5	
8.	1985-86	28,311	19,625	7,848	55,784	35.8	
9.	1986-87	28,205	19,400	7,848	55,453	35.6	
10.	1987-88	2,396	19,381	7,871	55,648	35.7	
11.	1988-89	28.159	19.424	7,664	55,247	35.5	
12.	1989-90	28,015	19,457	7,639	55,111	35.4	
13.	1990-91	27.087.3	16,113.3 (D.P.) 13,967.0 (UDP)	15.9	57,183.6	36.7	D.P.: Demarcated Protected.
14.	1991-92	26,731.19	15,867.65 (D.P.) 14,212.71 (UDP)	16.03	56,827.58	36.5	U.D.P.: Undemarcated Protected

Source : 1. *Statistical Abstracts of Orissa-1977*, O.G.P., 1980, p. 138.
2. *Statistical Abstracts of Orissa-1981*, O.G.P., 1985, p. 242.
3. *Statistical Abstracts of Orissa-1991*, O.G.P., 1991, p. 52.
4. *Economic Survey*. *1991-92*, O.G.P., 1992, p. 184.
5. *Economic Survey*, *1992-93*, O.G.P., 1993, p. 159.

TABLE 6.3 : Land Utilisation Pattern in Undivided Koraput District

(*Figures in '000 Hectares*)

Sl.No.	*Land-use category*	*1960-61*	*1975-76*	*1980-81*	*1985-86*	*1986-87*	*1987-88*	*1988-89*	*1989-90*
1	*2*	*3*	*4*	*5*	*6*	*7*	*8*	*9*	*10*
1.	Geographical area	2,554	2,702	2,702	2,702	2,702	2,702	2,702	2,702
2.	Forest Area	493 (19.30)	1,480 (54.77)	1,400 (51.81)	1,230 (45.52)	901 (33.35)	901 (33.35)	901 (33.35)	887 (32.83)
3.	Misc. tree crops and groves not included in net sown area	206 (8.07)	52 (1.92)	91 (3.37)	150 (5.55)	241 (8.92)	241 (8.92)	241 (8.92)	234 (8.66)
4.	Permanent pasture and other grazing lands	125 (4.89)	57 (2.12)	94 (3.48)	104 (3.85)	160 (5.92)	160 (5.92)	160 (5.92)	160 (5.92)
5.	Culturable waste/ Cultivable waste	231 (9.04)	34 (1.26)	30 (1.11)	85 (3.15)	106 (3.92)	106 (3.92)	106 (3.92)	196 (7.25)
6.	Land put to non-agricultural uses, not available for cultivation	250 (9.79)	—	94 (3.48)	110 (4.07)	142 (5.26)	142 (5.26)	142 (5.26)	161 (5.96)
7.	Barren and unculturable land	384 (15.04)	125 (4.63)	45 (1.66)	122 (4.52)	205 (7.59)	205 (7.59)	205 (7.59)	205 (7.59)
8.	Current fallows	59 (2.31)	88 (3.25)	65 (2.41)	59 (2.18)	68 (2.51)	86 (3.18)	68 (2.51)	31 (1.15)
9.	Other fallows	12 (0.47)	45 (1.67)	20 (0.74)	73 (2.70)	119 (4.40)	119 (4.40)	119 (4.40)	68 (2.52)
10.	Net area shown	794 (31.09)	821 (30.38)	863 (31.94)	769 (28.46)	760 (28.13)	742 (27.46)	760 (28.13)	760 (28.12)

Source : 1. Government of Orissa, Bureau of Statistics & Economics, Orissa, Bhubaneswar : *Statistical Abstract of Orissa-1963*, O.G.P., 1967, pp. 581-93, Column-3.

2. *Statistical Abstracts of Orissa-1977*, O.G.P., 1980, pp. 58-60, column-4.

3. Govt. of Orissa, Directorate of Agriculture & Food Production, Orissa, Bhubaneswar : *Orissa Agricultural Statistics-1980-81, 1985-86, 1986-87 and 1989-90.*

TABLE 6.4 · Land Utilisation Pattern in Orissa

(Figures in '000 hectares)

Sl.No.	*Land-use category*	*1950-51*	*1955-56*	*1960-61*	*1970-71*	*1975-76*	*1980-81*
1	*2*	*3*	*4*	*5*	*6*	*7*	*8*
1.	Geographical area	15,579 (100)	15,572 (100)	15,540 (100)	15,540	15,540	15,540 (100)
2.	Forest area	2,899 (18.61)	3,536 (22.71)	3,566 (22.95)	6,088 (39.18)	6,359 (40.92)	6,640 (42.73)
3.	Miscellaneous Tree crops and groves (not included in net sown area).	—	463 (2.96)	461 (2.97)	616 (3.96)	491 (3.16)	423 (2.72)
4.	Permanent pasture other grazing lands.	—	736 (4.73)	737 (4.74)	537 (3.46)	537 (3.46)	560 (3.60)
5.	Culturable wastes/ Cultivable waste	3,009 (19.31)	1,418 (9.11)	1,349 (8.68)	512 (3.29)	356 (2.29)	249 (1.60)
6.	Land put to non-agricultural uses. (Not available for cultivation)	3,009 (19.31)	1,100 (7.06)	1,143 (7.36)	840 (5.40)	880 (5.66)	632 (4.07)
7.	Barren and uncultivable land (Not available for cultivation)	—	1,439 (9.24)	1,399 (9.00)	—	—	265 (1.70)
8.	Current Fallows	—	—	915 (5.89)	1,075 (6.92)	555 (3.57)	452 (2.91)
9.	Other Fallows	1,005 (6.45)	1,155 (7.42)	183 (1.17)	270 (1.74)	225 (1.45)	189 (1.22)
10.	Net area sown	5,657 (36.32)	5,603 (35.98)	5,787 (37.24)	5,602 (36.05)	6,137 (39.49)	6,130 (39.45)

(Contd.)

TABLE 6.4 (*Contd.*)

Sl.No.	*Land-use category*		*1985-86*	*1986-87*	*1987-88*	*1988-89*	*1989-90*	*1990-91*
1	*2*		*9*	*10*	*11*	*12*	*13*	*14*
1.	Geographical area		15,540	15,540	15.540	15.540	15.540	15.540
2.	Forest area		5,955 (38.32)	5,579 (35.90)	5,579 (35.90)	5,583 (35.93)	5,476 (35.24)	5,476 (35.24)
3.	Miscellaneous Tree crops and groves (not included in net sown area).		619 (3.98)	719 (4.63)	719 (4.63)	716 (4.61)	859 (5.52)	859 (5.53)
4.	Permanent pasture other grazing lands.		618 (3.98)	711 (4.58)	711 (4.58)	726 (4.67)	726 (4.67)	726 (4.67)
5.	Culturable wastes/ Cultivable waste		403 (2.59)	463 (2.98)	463 (2.98)	444 (2.86)	517 (3.33)	597 (3.84)
6.	Land put to non-agricultural uses.	Not available for cultivation	688 (4.43)	723 (4.65)	723 (4.65)	723 (4.65)	742 (4.77)	746 (4.80)
7.	Barren and uncultivable land		367 (2.36)	450 (2.90)	450 (2.90)	450 (2.90)	499 (3.21)	499 (3.21)
8.	Current Fallows		218 (1.40)	275 (1.76)	620 (3.99)	262 (1.68)	146 (0.94)	119 (0.77)
9.	Other Fallows		349 (2.25)	353 (2.27)	321 (2.06)	356 (2.29)	254 (1.65)	214 (1.38)
10.	Net area sown		6,323 (40.69)	6,267 (40.33)	5,954 (38.31)	6,280 (40.41)	6,321 (40.67)	6.304 (40.56)

Source : 1. Govt. of Orissa, State Planning Machinery, Planning & Co-Ordination Department : Plan Information, Vol. III. O.G.P. 1983, p. 16 (cols. 3, 6 and 9).
2. Bureau of Statistics & Economics, Bhubaneswar : *Statistical Abstract of Orissa, 1963*, O.G.P. 1967. pp. 581-93 (cols. 4 and 5).
3. Bureau of Statistics and Economics, Bhubaneswar : *Statistical Abstracts of Orissa, 1977*, O.G.P. 1980. pp. 57-59 (cols. 7, 8 and 9);
4. Directorate of Economics & Statistics, Orissa, Bhubaneswar : *Statistical Abstract, 1991*, O.G.P. 1991, pp. 17-18 (cols. 10 to 13).
5. Directorate of Agriculture & Food Production, Orissa, Bhubaneswar : *Orissa Agricultural Statistics, 1989-90*, A.I.S.. Bhubaneswar, 1992, col. 14.
6. Planning & Co-Ord. Department, *Economics Survey, 1992-93*, O.G.P. 1993, pp. 146-47, col. 15.

TABLE 6.5 : Forest Revenue and Forest Expenditure in Koraput District.

(*Rs. in lakhs*)

Year	Revenue	Expenditure	Surplus
1983-84	489.75	184.29	305.46
1984-85	434.38	144.05	290.33
1985-86	659.22	158.95	500.54
1986-87	646.54	188.68	457.86
1987-88	630.86	270.34	420.52

Source: District Administration, Koraput, Koraput District: A Profile, December, 1988.

On the other hand due to the gradual regulation of rights and privileges of tribals in the forest policies enunciated from time to time, tribals find it more difficult to meet their requirements and find themselves alien on their own land.

Strategy of National Forest Policy, 1988

It would be desirable to examine the strategy of 1988 Forest Policy at a greater length to appreciate it in a better way.

A major finding of the above analysis of the forest policy is that these policies have failed to harness the tremendous attachment the tribals have for the forests for their own development. It would be desirable to enlist the cooperation of the tribals for preservation and management of forests by establishing a nexus between their welfare and the forest department.

It is, however, encouraging to note that the National Forest Policy, 1988 has tried to build up a sound strategy which if properly shaped and implemented will sort out many difficulties faced by us earlier.

Besides calling for a massive need-based and time bound programme of afforestation and tree planting, the policy has emphasised to encourage planting of trees along side of roads, railways lines, rivers, streams and canals. It has noted to take up development of tree crops and fodder resources on the village and community lands as well as on lands not required for productive uses. (Govt. of India, 1988, 4.2). The revenue generated through such programmes should belong to the Panchayats where the lands are vested in them, and in all other cases, the revenue should be shared with the local communities, in order to provide an incentive to them. The policy has given definite emphasis to ensure usufruct right to the beneficiaries over trees and in turn to make them responsible for their security and maintenance. It has also called for modification of land laws to facilitate and motivate individuals and institutions to undertake tree forming and grow fodder plants, grasses and legumes on their own land. The policy has also noted that degraded lands can be made available for tree-farming either on lease or on the basis of tree *patta*, scheme subject to the land grant rules and land ceiling laws.

In order to meet the growing needs of essential goods and services which the forests provide, the policy has suggested application of scientific and technical inputs, to enhance forest cover and productivity. The policy has taken care to encourage native tree species which have been tried for centuries and have been found suitable and is spectical about introduction of exotic species (Government of India, 1988, 4.3).

The policy has been careful to deal with the tribals in a friendly tone while discussing about their customary rights and concessions. The policy has recognised the grazing rights but has called for encouragement of stall feeding. It has taken care to give full protection of rights and concessions of the tribals living within and near forests. It has called for relieving the pressure on forests for the demand of railway sleepers and construction industry (particularly in the public sector). In order to meet with the problems of 'fuel-wood', it has emphasised on poplularisation of fuel efficient 'chullahs', bio-gas, L.P.G. and solar energy.

Realising the already aggravated problems of development versus displacement, the policy has emphasised careful examinations by specialists from the standpoint of social and environmental costs and benefits, for diversion of forest land for non-forest purposes even if it means construction of public projects. In order to discourage shifting cultivation practices, the policy has recognised the need for alternative means of livelihood. It has also recognised the need for encouragement of tribal cooperatives, labour co-operatives, government cooperations etc. to check illegal felling of trees by contractors. In order to meet with the problems of raw material shortage of forest based industries, the policy has emphasised that, "a forest based industry should raise the raw material needed for meeting its own requirements".

Adequate attention has been paid for personal management, forest research and financial support for forestry.

However, there are some important issues which have not been given due consideration in the National Forest Policy, 1988. Large extent of forest land which is under the possession and cultivation of tribals are still treated as encroachment cases. The Government of Orissa has made a policy decision to regularise pre-1980 encroachments and not to regularise post-1980 encroachments to discourage further encroachment. The existing laws relating to forest land still act as obstacles to make the policy decisions a practicable proposition.

Similarly, due to the various restrictions imposed by Forest Conservation Act, in many cases the inhabitants of forest villages are deprived of getting the fruits of development planning. These inhabitants cannot even construct school buildings, dispensaries and the like due to these restrictions.

Over the years it has been experienced by all of us that ensuring usufruct right to the beneficiaries has not been able to make them responsible for the protection and maintenance of trees. Hence, the policy of making degraded land available for tree farming either on the basis of lease or tree *patta* needs careful consideration.

It would be desirable to give ownership right to individual tribal families for encouraging tree farming on the degraded lands to enlist their full support in the protection, regeneration and development of forest. The existing laws relating to forest land need to be changed to regularise forest land encroachment cases. If a tribal family is able to get good crops from the cultivation of forest land, it is worthwhile to allot the land in his favour and confer ownership right on him rather than treating it as encroachment, whether it is a pre-1980 or post 1980 case.

This New Forest Policy of 1988 appears to be realistic in its approach. However, the success of the policy depends more on the 'political will', practical and accommodative attitude of forest officials, voluntary agencies and sincerity of people at large'.

REFERENCES

Abreo Desmond D., *People and Forests (1982)*, Indian Social Institute, New Delhi.

Govt. of India, *National Forest Policy, 1988.*

Mohapatro, P.C. and S.C. Patnaik, *Tribal Development in a Forestry Framework: A Case Study of Koraput District (1984) in Rural Development Strategies for Weaker Sections*, Ed. K. Prasad *et al.*,—Puspagiri Press, Cuttack.

Padhi, G.S., *Forest Resources of Orissa (1984)*, Udyog Printers, Bhubaneswar.

Sagreiya, K.P., *Forests and Forestry, 1982*, National Book Trust, India.

Sharad Kulkarni, *The Forest Policy and Forest Bill: A Critique and Suggestions for Change in Towards a New Forest Policy, 1988*, (ed.), Walter Fernandes, *et al.*

Walter Fernandes, *Forest Policy: A Solution to Tribal Deprivation, 1992* in National Development and Tribal Deprivation, (ed.), Walter Fernandes.

7

PODU
An Ecological Hazard

— *C.R. Mohapatra*

Orissa is mainly an agrarian State with 80 per cent of its population living in villages. The way of life, the culture, the arts and the crafts and the occupation of the bulk of the people lean heavily on forestry and innumerable products derived therefrom. This very dependence makes forests invaluable for the people in India. Heavy pressures of human and cattle population have led to the disappearance of forests from densely populated areas. The biggest single demand that the community places on forests is for fuelwood. This demand is estimated to be nearly 150 million tonnes while the recorded production of fuelwood is nearly 16 million tonnes. Owing to great shortage of fuelwood and in the absence of alternative sources of energy, cowdung which is a good and cheap manure is burnt as fuel. The diversion of cowdung from the field to the hearth has led to poor agricultural yields. Besides fuelwood, the forests have to provide fodder for cattle, wood for house construction and agricultural implements and gainful employment to the rural population. The disappearance of forests from rural areas has brought about a crisis in rural economy.

The Forest of Orissa is the abode of the 62 different tribes speaking 25 different tribal languages. The tribal population in State are more than 25 lakhs, about 25 per cent of the total population of the State, Juanga, Gadaba, Paraja, Bonda, Didayi, Koya, Binjhia, Bhumija Saoras, Kondh, Bhuyan, Gond are some of the important groups of tribals. Many tribals speak Oriya with local dialectical variations. None of the tribal languages referred to above belong to two linguistic families namely Mundari group of the Austro-Asiatic sub-family and the South Dravidian, sub-group of the Dravidian family of languages. Amongst the tribals 61 per cent are engaged as cultivators, 21 per cent agricultural labourers, 18 per cent get themselves engaged in Forestry, Mining, Fishing and Hunting, etc. Rests are engaged in miscellaneous profession. Hunting for the tribals of Orissa is more of a sport and cultural pastime than a source of income ceremonial hunting marks the communal feeling of the tribals. With the progressive diminution of forest and restrictions enforced by law the tribals seldom go on hunting expedition. From the economic point of view the tribals of Orissa may be classified under three categories. First type, the Kharias who are semi-nomadic; work out their living mainly by collection of honey, roots and tubers, silk cocoons and other forest produce. The second type are Hill Juangas, Pauri, Bhuiyans, Kutia, Kondhas and Lanjia Saoras practise shifting cultivation (*Podu*) and supplement their economy by food collection. The third type is the settled cultivators/agriculturists. The tribals in different economic stages also exhibit varying stages of cultural development.

Podu cultivation is also known as *Jhum* or shifting cultivation. It has got its wide extension all over Asia. This *podu* cultivation can be identified as : (i) Active, (ii) Dormant or pseudo active, and (iii) extinct.

Normally though people call the practice of *Podu* as shifting cultivation yet I would call it as "Rotating cultivation". The process of "shifting" is only a temporary action because after a lapse of 5 to 10 years period the tribals again resume the cultivation they left over. Thus, the cultivation goes on in a cyclic manner with variable time gap. One appreciates the strong understanding amongst the tribals as hardly there is any dispute for encroachment or unrecognised authority of ownership on a piece of land. As regards to the classification of Active-Dormant-Extinct, the area where *podu* cultivation is continuing at present may be classified under the category "Active". The second category of land is under rest and is awaiting cultivation after a lapse of few years. But the land under third category is the gone case where no further cultivation can be taken up.

What do they do? The tribals either makes clear felling of a particular patch of forest burn the vegetative growth and then start hoeing operation before sowing of their agricultural crop or at times they girdle the trees for a natural death of the trees after which the operation of felling and burning becomes easier for them. Continuously for three years the tribals carry on cultivation thereafter they shift to another patch. But, again after an interval of 10/12 years depending upon the availability of forest area they come back to the left over area and re-do the past operation. Hence during the lean period when there is no on-going activity the "*Podu* area" remains almost "dormant". But due to repeated cultivation i.e., unscientific way of disturbing the soil, there occurs soil erosion resulting in exposure of either parent rock or the soil does not possess any fertility due to which the area is left over further to be eroded. This type of area is classified as "Extinct".

Causes—Practising of *podu* cultivation is not an abnormal practice. It is the normal human instinct and the desire to survive. The only negative factor attributed is the "primitive method". The practising of "*podu*" can be differentiated further as absolute-induced and accused.

(i) *Absolute*—Under this category the tribals carry on the practice as an age old tradition.

(ii) *Induced*—The outside unscrupulous money lender volunteer to lend money to the tribals and induce them to carry on with an understanding, take a lion share of the produce as "interest". The outstanding capital remains as heavy burden on the tribals and also ultimately engages the tribals as 'bonded labourer'.

(iii) *Accused*—Under this category some of the anti-social elements exercise their unauthorised influence to lure the Adivasis with a false hope to record the land in the name of the cultivators. But ultimately the cultivator is being accused as an offenders.

The cumulative effect of *Podu* cultivation can not be quantified in monetary terms. It has done harm to foresters, to agriculturists, to biologists, to many others. In totality it has changed our 'Environment', The depletion of vegetation has had its impact both on micro flora, fauna and climate.

This malady of *Podu* cultivation is an age old practice. It started with the birth of human race. It continued and may continue for years to come. It cannot be stopped. But the intelligentsia who express concern about the deterioration of our environment should think and act to arrest the process if not stop it. It is not a problem confined only to few specific department of the Government organization. The people who are the real beneficiaries need to be motivated and their active and sustained interest has got to be ensured. These requirements call for the establishment of new institutions and the adoption of a relevant forestry technology. An effective forestry extension organisation is very necessary to propagate the idea of community forestry and to convince the villagers that their welfare is intimately linked with it. This is not an easy task. The extension personnel should have sound knowledge of socio-economic problems of the community and of human behaviours. The present forestry organisations in the State are deficient in this respect. Realizing their shortcomings extension courses for forest officers drafted for implementing these programmes are being organised with the help of Agricultural Universities.

Motivation of the rural masses is the most important single factor in determining the success of such a programme. Long gestation period of forestry programmes is an important handicap in obtaining people's participation.

A programme of reafforestation combined with wood gasification will restore agriculture to its original place as the base of all subsequent transformation activity in the economy in particular, it will largely replace fossil fuels as the sources of highly concentrated forms of energy. As a result, a large part of the enormous increased in productivity that are taking place in industry will be funnelled back directly into the rural areas, where four out of five people live.

Perhaps the most attractive feature of a development strategy based on reafforestation is that its implementation requires no radical shift in the patterns of investment that has been pursued in the country so far. For instance, while it will profoundly alter the energy base of the economy, it will require no change in the Industrial "Superstructure" that has been build on it.

Since synthetic gas (carbon monoxide and hydrogen), the basic product of wood gasification can meet each and every need of the petrochemicals industry even more easily than natural gas, none of the petrochemicals plants that are now being built all over the country will be rendered obsolete. What is more, since all the end products of this industry will remain available even when oil finally runs out, no change in life styles will be called for.

There is no need to create new institution to finance social forestry loans. The banking system—both commercial and co-operative banks can do this by hypothecating the standing tree crop and relating the annual advance to the number of trees still standing (in practice it is most unlikely that many will die after the first year or two of life). The reluctance that many banks feel about loans against standing crops, even of a non-perishable kind like trees, can be overcome by setting up a refinance or guarantee corporation to underwrite such loans, in fact the newly created NABARD (National Apex Bank for Agriculture and Rural Development) is already underwriting loans for forestry, but only those given to institutions and not to individuals. It is, therefore, only a tiny steps away from the desired goal of becoming a full fledged refinancing corporation for Forest Development. Shortening the gestation period can help in ensuring their interest and participation. In traditional forestry, the benefits start accruing only at the thinning stage which may take 5 to 10 years. Such species as can ensure returns in 2 or 3 years have now been selected for community forestry programmes. This approach has paid a rich devidend in many areas where willing co-operation of the people has been ensured. Besides this the decision that the revenue accruing from the rural forestry programmes would be shared with the rural community based on the recommendation of the National Commission on Agriculture has also been very helpful.

Afforestation and plantation programmes assume great importance to enrich the forest wealth of the State and to cater to the demands of small timber as well as firewood requirements of the State. There are number of hydroelectric projects and irrigation projects. It is necessary to give an adequate vegetative cover to the catchment areas of these projects in order to control soil erosion and arrest the rapid siltation of the reservoirs. Large areas of the forest land have been denuded due to the extensive practice of shifting cultivation. All these factors demand greater attention to the afforestation and deforestation programmes.

The involvement of the people has to be right from the formulation stage of these programmes and should also be a sustained one. The programmes are required to be formulated in consultation with the people. The beginning is made by holding dialogues with the local leaders. They are to be explained that these programmes are being executed for their welfare and all the benefits will accrue to them. Extension wings have been created in Forest Departments of some States for this purpose.

The implementation of the forestry for the people programmes requires a strong research backing. Some of the problems requiring research investigations are the interaction of trees and agricultural crops, the role of trees in ecological balance of the region, selection of suitable species for different agro-climatic and edaphic zones, selection and breeding of fast growing and superior genotypes, collection, processing and marketing of different products to be obtained from community forestry and research in extension methods. Research on some of these problems has been initiated at some agricultural universities and research centres of the Forest Research Institute.

In view of the overwhelming dependence of the rural community in general and of the tribals in particular on the forests and forest products, the interaction between communities and forests is pronounced. Briefly stated, the stability of the rural community in turn depends upon proper maintenance of the forests. Unfortunately in this country the forests have not been well treated by the rural communities which have been meeting their basic forest-based needs without any thought to forest replenishment or whether the forest can meet these requirements in perpetuity. The consequence has been the widespread destruction of forests all over the country. To ensure people's participation a new approach totally different from the traditional ones need to be adopted. It needs scientists, sociologist, politicians and elites of the society to sit together and plan out plausible solutions to the problems. During last 40 years under different tribal development schemes attempts have been made to improve upon their socio-economic condition. Permanent settlement, i.e., Housing schemes and provision of cultivable land were made to bring them down the hills. Improved varieties of cattle were supplied to the adivasis. Training was arranged for the youth to take up different types of vocation. Attempts do continue to improve upon their health and hygiene.

When there is scarcity of cultivable land can we implement a land consolidation system and distribute for their permanent cultivation? Will they accept it? Who will implement— they by themselves or through Government or semi-Government media? Fuelwood scarcity has stood as a grave problem for all common man who depend upon the tribals to collect firewood for them. Thus can we stop illicit fellings? Evil effects of *podu* cultivation should be taught to the forest dwellers. Can they be taught in a befitting manner? Who will teach them our literacy percentage as a whole in the State stands at 34 per cent. Many schemes and projects have been taken up in the tribal areas why did they not make appreciable impact on their development? These are some of the burning thoughts which should be dealt in detail and action plan be prepared as remedial measures. It is thought provoking, why not let the stream flow its own course. Thereby, I do not suggest to encourage further shifting cultivation. I do visualise only a corrective method to keep the flow of the stream within its two banks. The idea is only a symbiosis. Forestry and continuance of shifting cultivation is proposed to be taken up in parallel lines. My little experience shows that through Agro silvicultural method it has been possible to persuade the adivasis gradually to change their mind. It is difficult for the *podu* cultivators to leave their "profession", to shed off the superstition, the age old tradition embedded to their life style. It would be a blunder on the part of the civilized city dwelling brothers to crode the habits , the habitants particularly the rich heritage of their culture. We may try to educate them, provide better amenities and comforts to enjoy a better living condition, but not at the cost of their own identity. Seldom an Indian can adopt the philosophy and life style of an European. Because an Indian is an Indian born and brought up under a different environment, having the variable components such as weather, food habits, different tradition and religious philosophy. Thus, a forest, dweller cannot be converted to urbanisation. Everything, that requires to stop the practice of shifting cultivation and change the mind of the beneficiary is a devoted and dedicated machinery that will act in a concentrated manner instead of a diffused action. In the words of Shri Kuldip Nayar "Seminars are as a rule dull. Their very nature makes them so. The only speeches are the inaugural and validictory ones. The rest of the time is taken by papers, which are read. The most impact any paper can aspire to create is to be described lively".

8

SHIFTING CULTIVATION AND ITS IMPACT ON FOREST ECO-SYSTEM

— *K. Nana Buchi*

I

Forests are one of the most important natural resources of the State of Orissa. Forests are rich in timber and fire-wood, and are a source of good minor forest products. During 1988-89, the State earned Rs. 24.95 crores and Rs. 34.23 crores from major and minor forest products respectively.[1] Table 8.1 reveals the total forest area of the State during 1978-79, 1988-89 and 1990-91.

TABLE 8.1 : Geographical Area and Forest Area of the State of Orissa

(*'000 Hectares*)

Sl. No.	*Year*	*Total geographical area*	*Forest area*	*Percentage of col. 4 to col. 3*
1	*2*	*3*	*4*	*5*
1.	1978-79	15,540	6,655	42.8
2.	1988-89	15,540	5,583	35.9
3.	1990-91	15,540	5,476	35.2

Source : *Orissa Agricultural Statistics, 1978-79, 1988-89* and 1990-91, Directorate of Agricultural and Food Production, Bhubaneswar, Orissa, (Figures compiled).

It is noticed that the forest area of the State was 42.8 per cent of the total geographical area in 1978-79. It came down to 35.2 per cent in 1990-91 due to destruction of forests by men and animals. Urbanisation and industrialisation are the main causes of loss of forest area. Added to it, the other cause, in the Sub-Plan areas of the State, is shifting cultivation.

Shifting cultivation in Orissa is also known as "*Podu*" or "*Bagada*" or "*Jhum*" cultivation. It is an age-old practice of the tribes who inhabit the hill-tops or hill-slopes. It is part of the customs and the traditions of the tribals of the State. The total area under shifting cultivation and the number of tribes engaged are shown in Table 8.2.

TABLE 8.2 : Total Area and Number of Tribes Engaged in Shifting Cultivation in Orissa

Sl. No.	*Year*	*Source of estimation*	*No. of tribals depending on shifting cultivation & their percentage to total tribal population*	*Total area of forest land affected & their percentage to total forest (in acres)*
1	*2*	*3*	*4*	*5*
1.	1951	F.M. Mooney	9,33,500 (53.5%)	81,72,800 (53.6%)
2.	1956	Indian Council of Agricultural Research	10,00,000 (33.7%)	4,00,000 (2.6%)
3.	1960-61	Commissioner for SC & ST	9,35,700	4,00,000
4.	1971-72	D.F.O., Forest Research Survey, Orissa	10,00,000 (19.7%)	34,59,400 (20.8%)
5.	1972-73	Tribal & Harijan Research-cum-Training Institute, Orissa	2,40,000 (4.7%)	46,500 (0.3%)
6.	1975	Director of Agriculture, Orissa, Erts-I, Sattelite Imagery	—	81,72,800 (49.7%)

Source : Mohapatra, P.C., "Economic Development of Tribal India", Ashish Publishing House, New Delhi, 1987, p. 134.

The area under shifting cultivation varies from one estimation to other. Taking into account the estimates made by Mooney (1951) and the Director of Agriculture, Orissa (1975), it is noticed that the total area affected by shifting cultivation was 81.7 lakh acres in Orissa. As per the survey conducted by the Soil Survey Wing, it has been estimated that 1.85 lakh hactares have been affected annually in Orissa by shifting cultivation.[2] In Orissa, this is in practice among the Kutia-Kondh, Dongria Kondh of Koraput and Phulbani, the Koya, Bonda and Gadaba of Koraput, Lanjia-Soura of Ganjam and Koraput, the Kondh and Pengo-Kondh of Kalahandi, and the Juang and Paudi Bhuyan of Keonjhar district.[3]

Under this type of cultivation, a patch of forest is cleared on a hill-slope during January and March. During, April, the waste materials are burnt and the ashes are spread evenly on the ground. After that the seeds are spread over the area. The crops are harvested during September and December of the same year. The tribes adopt mixed cropping under this type of cultivation. They raise crops like Ragi, Jowar, Castor, Arhar, Kangu etc. The tribals take up shifting cultivation in cycle varying from 8 to 12 years.[4]

The shifting cultivation is wasteful and of low productive value. The average yield from one acre of *podu* land is 200 Kgs. besides 100 kgs. of creeper grains, whereas in low lying area of plains, the average yield per acre varies from 640 kgs. to 800 Kgs.[5] Taking into account the labour involved in it, the income from *podu* cultivation is 1/3 or 1/4 of the total cost of production.[6]

This type of cultivation has devastating effects, as it causes springs below the hills to dry up, degrades the forest area, washes away fertile soil land ruins valuable timber and other forest resources of the State. The hill ranges present a barren and dismal look with poor or no forest growth. On the top of it all, the effect of shifting cultivation is more pronounced on the ecosystem.

II

The forest ecosystem consists of major components like atmosphere, climate, soil and its living organisms. They influence the environmental quality of the earth. The living organisms (plants and animals) maintain a balance between carbon-dioxide and oxygen in the atmosphere. The plants, as primary producers, utilise the carbondioxide as raw material and releases oxygen to the atmosphere. On the other hand, the animals utilise the oxygen and give off carbondioxide. This balance is disturbed as the tribes set fire to the forest for clearing the ground for the purpose of cultivation. This results, on one hand, in increase of the quantity of carbondioxide in the atmosphere, and on the other, in the large scale destruction of plants and trees, the main utilisers of this poisonous gas. As a result, the temperature of the earth increases. This also affects the wild life. Shifting cultivation not only affects the plants and animals, but also the tribes who are living in the forests and are an important organism in the forest ecosystem.

The deforestation caused by *podu* cultivation also reduces the normal rainfall. It is noticed that due to increase of temperature in the atmosphere, rainfall in many years decreases in comparison to the normal rainfall of the State. It also changes the character and composition of the forest ecosystem.

In addition to deforestation, shifting cultivation leads to soil erosion due to loss of complete or partial destruction of natural vegetation. The fertility of the soil decreases due to the loss of surface and sub-soil as it is exposed to wind and water. It also decreases the water-holding and the retaining capacity of the soil.

From the above, it is clear that the environment which is the aggregate of biotic and abiotic factors, is polluted due to imbalance between carbondioxide and oxygen, increase in dust and temperature, decrease in humidity, reduction in rainfall, varying climatic conditions, and spread of plant and animal diseases.

Man as a living organism has to depend upon its environment. So the man and the environment are two non-separable factors. Man as a important consumer of plant and its product, should not destroy forests for mere cultivation like shifting cultivation, which is also not profitable. Further, pollution due to deforestation is so widespread and substantial that the very existence of life on the earth is threatened. If sufficient steps are not taken to prevent *podu* cultivation, and pollution, even the entire earth, it is feared, may not be suitable for human habitation.

III

The evil effects of shifting cultivation have been recognised for the last many years. Various authorities and Committees have gone into it, and made various recommendations. All have unanimously expressed the view that measures to stop shifting cultivation or to eliminate it to the best possible extent, should be taken up without any loss of time.

The National Forest Policy, 1952 stressed that "Possibility of regulating shifting cultivation by combining it with forest regeneration to the benefit of both should be fully explored".[7] The National Commission on Agriculture, 1976 viewed that "shifting cultivation should be regulated, controlled and replaced as expeditiously as possible by resorting to agri-silvicultural methods apart from other methods. This should be explored, planned and implemented, in co-operation with other concerned departments. But regulation of shifting cultivation should form a part of a wider plan for the tribal welfare".[8] The State Forest Enquiry Committee recommended that "(a) the *podu* tribals should be moved to settled agriculture and colonies where they should be given facilities of irrigation, agricultural implements, bullocks, etc.,

(b) controlled *podu* on hill-tops be allowed, (c) the forested area should be replanted with cashew, coffee, bamboos etc".[9]

It is also recommended by the Committee on Forest and Tribals in India, that as shifting cultivation has become a way of life with the tribals, change from such cultivation to settled cultivation must be gradual. They are to be motivated by introducing alternative programmes. The Committee also recommended that—(a) special comprehensive projects for each micro situation with problem of shifting cultivation as their focus should be prepared and they should be induced to switch over to settled cultivation; (b) the settlement of such cultivators should primarily be within the area of their traditional habitat; (c) comprehensive micro-plans for each group of cultivators should be prepared by inter-disciplinary teams which may be constituted exclusively for this purpose; (d) land which are freed from shifting cultivation should be used immediately without any time-lag; and (e) there should be effective evaluation and monitoring of the programme.[10]

In the State of Orissa, the Government have already implemented a large number of schemes and programmes as measured to control shifting cultivation. Colonies were set up since 1948-49 to settle the tribes and were provided with lands for cultivation. During the Fifth Five Year Plan, the State government formulated a special scheme for rehabilitation of 20 thousand *podu* families at an estimated cost of Rs. 1285 crores. Under this scheme, the Government proposed to provide one hectare of land for horticulture and one unit of animal husbandry per *podu* family residing in higher slopes, and 2 acres of reclaimed land, input assistance and animal husbandry component per each such family residing in lower slopes.[11]

As soil erosion is an acute problem, the Soil Conservation Department of the State has implemented different conservative programmes like bunding and terracing, plantation of quick growing fruit trees on hill slopes, construction of check dams and water-harvesting structures to protect land from gully erosion.[12]

Besides resettlement and soil conservation measures, the Government have also implemented schemes like development of horticulture, afforestation, introduction of cash crops like cashewnut, coffee, etc. and animal husbandry in the *podu* affected areas of the State.

During 1984-85, the State government launched a programme for rehabilitation of *podu* cultivators out of the special grant to the State under Article 275(1) of the Constitution of India. Accordingly the forest department of the State drew a 5 year Perspective Plan Programme to be implemented in the State. But the State government decided to implement the said programme through the I.T.D.As. of the sub-plan areas. Similarly, in the year 1987-88, the National Government introduced another scheme to control shifting cultivation. This scheme aims at implementing location-specific viable schemes. So the government had drawn up 10 micro-projects covering 183 villages spread over 6 district with a target of 6181 *podu* families for settlement.

Inspite of the above, shifting cultivation is still being practised widely in the districts of Koraput, Ganjam, Phulbani and Keonjhar on a large scale. The tribals take up this type of cultivation due to their illiteracy and as a culture and traditional occupation. It is revealed that the tribes who are residing on the foot-hills, and and having plain lands for cultivation, cultivate *podu* on the hill-tops and slopes as a traditional practice. Therefore, it is suggested that:

(1) As the tribes are illiterate, steps should be taken to educate them on the lines of settled cultivation, and convince them about the undesirability of *podu* and the advantages of the settled cultivation.

(2) Awareness of the consequences and hazards of *podu* cultivation is to be created in the mind of tribals, and they are to be motivated to conserve the forest and its wealth.

(3) Plantation of fruit-bearing trees should be done on a large scale in *podu*-affected area as the tribals respect the preserve fruit trees.

(4) In case of resettlement, they are to be provided sufficient employment opportunities to earn adequate income to maintain the family properly, so that they may not be interested to go back to their original place and resort again to *podu* cultivation.

(5) To attract the tribes towards settled cultivation, there should be timely provision of agricultural inputs such as seeds, fertilisers, irrigation facilities etc.

(6) Employment opportunities are to be created for the development of tribal women.

In conclusion, what is more important is to form a Committee in the District Planning Unit of tribal districts of the State to prepare a perspective district plan for controlling shifting cultivation. The District Level Committee, comprising the District Collector and other officials of other departments at the district level who are directly related to control *podu*, should first take up the task of identifying the *podu* families and the area affected. This is important in the sense that no clear picture has yet emerged about the *podu*-affected areas and the families. Different authorities have given different estimates (Table 8.2) on this issue. This will not serve the purpose. After collection of data, an integrated plan/programme is to be drawn up, and the dimension of the plan in terms of total effort required for each area should be clearly defined. Further, timely evaluation and monitoring should be taken up to make a success of the plan programmes.

NOTES

1. *Forestry in Orissa*, First Edition, Forest Department of Orissa, Bhubaneswar, pp. 6-7 (figures compiled).
2. Director of Soil Conservation, Government of Orissa, *Report No. 31*, No. 1.
3. Mohapatra, Kulamani and Dei Kiranabala: *Shifting Cultivation in Orissa, Adivasi*, Vol. XIV, 1972-73, No. 4, January 1973, p. 12.
4. *Sub-Plan for Tribal Regions of Orissa, 1974-79 (Draft)* Tribal & Rural Welfare Department, Government of Orissa, Bhubaneswar, p. 140.
5. Mohapatra, P.C. "Economic Development of Tribal India", *op. cit*, p. 144.
6. *I.T.D.A. Report*, Phulbani, Orissa, 1976, pp. 100-101.
7. Sub-Plan for Tribal Regions of Orissa, 1974-79, *op. cit.*, p. 140.
8. *Letter No. 3193/TDCCOL, dt. 3.4.84* of Managing Director, Tribal Dev. Cooperative Corporation of Orissa Ltd., Bhubaneswar to all Divisional Manager, TDCC, (Extract copy of the Report on National Commission on Agriculture, 1976).
9. Sub-Plan for Tribal Regions of Orissa, 1974-79, *op. cit.*, p. 140.
10. *Report of the Committee on Forest & Tribals in India*, Government of India, Ministry of Home Affairs, Tribal Development Division, New Delhi 1982, Chapter 8.
11. Mohapatra, P.C. "Economic Development of Tribal India", *op. cit.*, p. 146.
12. Tribal Sub-Plan for Eighth Plan, 1990-95 and Annual Sub-Plan, 1991-92, Orissa (Draft) Government of Orissa, H&TW Department, November 1990, p. 125.

9

IMPACT OF SHIFTING CULTIVATION ON FOREST ECO-SYSTEM

— *B.N. Thakur*

Introduction

The Shifting Cultivation, is a distinct type of agricultural practice generally practised in the hill slopes after sacrificing the forest cover standing over it. This type of cultivation is also known as *Podu* Cultivation and also as *Jhum* Cultivation in some parts of India. Such practice is not only limited to India alone but also followed by Yurba of Kongo basin, the Bemba of Northern Rhodesia, the Yao of Southern Nessa Land, the Boro of Western Amazan forest, the Bakairi Indians of Upper Xingu Region in South America etc. In Orissa this method is practised by Bonda, Paroja, Gadwa, Kutia Kondh, Dongria Kondh, Lanjia Soura, Juang Tribes etc.

Definitions and Evolutions

The shifting cultivation a primitive agricultural practice practised at the primitive level of operations under unconducive surroundings for a sustainable agriculture. In this process the cultivator first clears a chunk of good forest standing mostly on a hill slope. Almost all the tree species except fruit bearing species are cut at a stump height of 2' to 3' and then the branches as well as their lops and tops are burnt after they dried up. Then agricultural seeds are sown on this patch of land after a light soil preparation. During the initial two or three years good crops are harvested at a diminishing rate and then the land is abandoned until the hardy forest species recolonises the abandoned land into a renewed vegetation of inferior quality. This process continues until the land loses all its forces for recolonisation due to soil erosion, loss of fertility and soil exposure. Then the land is finally abandoned and a fresh clearing is invaded upon.

It is very difficult to ascertain the period at which this pernicious practice actually started. Some feel this practice to be as old as the humanity. From History it is evident that the pre-historic man were mostly leading nomadic life inside dense forest. Gradually they came to know about the agricultural practices and from that point of time the process of clearing forest for agriculture started which in course of time reached the stage of shifting cultivation. After resorting to agriculture most of the prehistoric man resorted to settled life whereas few conservatives moved as usual inside dense forest who had no other option than to practise shifting cultivation.

The practice of agriculture after scarificing forest was not felt in the olden days due to because the forest cover was plenty in comparison to population. So also was the case of shifting cultivation, which was being felt viable at that time.

Viability of Shifting Cultivation

The viability of shifting cultivation depends on few basic ingredients such as :

(a) Hill slopes covered with good forest cover,
(b) Timely rainfall,
(c) Limited tribal population preferring isolated forest life,
(d) Surplus forest land,
(e) Fixed and limited consumption needs,
(f) Scarce labour,
(g) Non-availability of capital resources.

Judging from the present day context all the above ingredients are not always available. The hill slopes are mostly barren after the forest cover has been lost, the rainfall is not always punctual, the tribal populations are always too many in comparison to the *podu* land available for them. In view of the above, the shifting cultivation is no more viable at the present day context and so the practice is felt pernicious now.

Extent of Shifting Cultivation in Orissa

No systematic study has so far been done to determine the exact area under shifting cultivation. Only some rough estimates are available from which we can know the area affected in different districts of Orissa are as follows :

TABLE 9.1 : Area affected in Different Districts of Orissa under Shifting Cultivation

Sl. No.	*District*	*Area under shifting cultivation in sq.km.*
1.	Ganjam	2,980
2.	Kalahandi	1,324
3.	Keonjhar	2,528
4.	Koraput	11,528
5.	Phulbani	8,435
6.	Sambalpur	1,913
7.	Sundargarh	2,270

Source : Harinath, C.M. (1990).

From the Table 9.1, it is evident that the area affected under *podu* is maximum in Koraput district. The report of shifting cultivation of Sri F.M. Mooney (1951) speaks about 8 tribes having a total population of 4,56,000 who practise shifting cultivation over 32,00,000 acres. The report of Orissa Forest Resources Survey (1971-72) speaks about 5,00,000 tribal population practising shifting cultivation over 14,82,000 acres of land. The above figures speak about the magnitude of the shifting cultivation in Orissa as well as in Koraput District alone.

Effects of Shifting Cultivation

Experts are divided on their opinion about the effects of shifting cultivation. Some feel that shifting cultivation is ruinous and wasteful to forest resources and environment. Whereas others like Sivaraman, Chaturvedi opined that shifting cultivation is not always harmful to the forest and the land as it can very well be improved and evil effects minimised by introducing leguminous crops and nitrogen fixing plantations as well as planting fruit-bearing trees by restricting *podu*.

If we analyse both the above views, we can come to the conclusion that the second view is nothing but supplementary to the first one, where the experts are affirmative of repairing the loss done to the forest by shifting cultivation through planting and introducing leguminous crops.

The present days forest are in a deteriorated condition due to human as well as cattle pressure which is no more capable of sustaining to the axe and fire of the shifting cultivators. Judging from the above perspective shifting cultivation affects the forest eco-system irreparably. The hill slopes are denuded and the soil is exposed to nature. The disturbance of top soil due to agricultural practice makes it more susceptible to erosion. Humus which covers the top soil is lost due to fire thereby reducing the water holding capacity and increasing runoff. The steep slope accelerates the carrying capacity of water and all the top soil is lost leaving behind gully, exposed rocks ravines. The loss of soil fertility and water level stops the recolonisation process for all times to come. The land which was once supporting good forest and wildlife becomes a heap of stone and exposed rocks. This not only affects environment but also the economy of other tribals who were once dependent on those forest for their timber and firewood requirements and M.F.P. collections.

Preventive Measures Taken Up

A number of programmes have been implemented both by the State as well as the Central Government under *Podu* Prevention Schemes. Some of them are :

(a) Land colonisation and settlement programmes,
(b) Horticultural plantation,
(c) Afforestation.

The rehabilitation of *podu* cultivators was launched during 1984-85 out of special grants of Central Government through I.T.D.As. In the year 1987-88 the Government of India introduced another scheme for control of shifting cultivation. Under the above schemes, the following sectoral development works were undertaken.

(1) Sisal plantation
(2) Cashew plantation
(3) Coffee plantation
(4) Horticulture
(5) Tree plantation
(6) Central Nursery
(7) Field bunding
(8) Bench terrace
(9) W.H.S.
(10) Orchards
(11) Gully control
(12) Land development
(13) Tube wells
(14) Communications
(15) L.I. Points
(16) Community Centres etc.

From the above programmes, it can be seen that except land colonisation and resettlement programmes all other programmes were oriented for the economic upliftment of the shifting cultivators. The land colonisation and resettlement was the only programme wherein the shifting cultivators were brought to specially built colonies for their resettlement, though the fate of those programmes are yet to be computed still then it can be said that yet more has to be done to stop the practice all-together.

Control Measures Suggested

The shifting cultivation is an age old practice which has been enshrined in the social ethos of the tribals who practise it. Thus, it is no doubt difficult but also time consuming to motivate the tribals to desist them from the above practice. Multidirectional approach when taken can only help in bringing the goal nearer and nearer. Location specific schemes are to be drawn after making detailed resources survey of each location. Some of the remedial measures suggested are as follows :

(1) *Rehabilitation Programmes*

Now being the shifting cultivation practices no more viable, some of the tribals have developed dis-interest to the practice but they are doing it on compulsion. Such persons through motivation can be brought down the hill slopes into rehabilitation colonies where they will be given all amenities for settled life. By making location-wise survey only such cases can be tapped.

(2) *Education Facility for their Children*

Steps are to be taken so that all the children of the shifting cultivators get education free so also the cultivators. Once they are educated they will lose interest for the above practice and as such from a particular generation it can be wiped out.

(3) *Viable Alternatives*

The remainder orthodox persons who neither opt for rehabilitation nor for education opportunities are to be given viable alternatives in their existing surroundings. Some such alternatives forecasted are :

(a) *Afforestation Programme :* These persons can be utilised in the afforestation programme in their *podu* areas. The afforestation programme need be so oriented so that work days/man days are generated throughout the year and along with wage they get food materials under World Food Programme Scheme.

(b) *Regulated Shifting Cultivation* : Selected few who opt for continuation of the above practice can also be engaged in a regulated type of shifting cultivation. In this method pollardable tree species will be raised at 5 Mtr. × 5 Mtr. or any convenient spacing and the interspace with quick growing species at a closure spacing. Each cultivator will be given 3 to 4 such plots. Each plot will be utilised for slush burn agriculture. In the first year quick growing species will be cut and in the second phase pollardable species will be cut at pollardable height after which he will shift to the next plot. In this process as the pollardable species will always stand, the soil will not be exposed completely. However, the effectiveness of this practice can be known only when tried in the field and the existing rule permits.

(c) *Auxiliary Activities* : These includes plantation of cash crop, herticultural species, terracing, bunding etc. which will ameliorate the economy of the tribals. But in the present conditions all the above activities are not allowed in the forest area under the Forest (Conservation) Act so also the shifting cultivation. On the other hand, such activities if done outside the forest area will not be of helpful to the shifting cultivators. In view of that before taking any such step in that direction, the legal aspect need be suitably interpreted so as to make it conducive for the purpose.

Conclusion

On analysis of the above, it is concluded that little has been done so far to achieve the stupendous task of weaning away shifting cultivation practices. By making whole-hearted approach starting from survey to planning out eradicative measures through location specific schemes will help find out easy and early solution of the problem.

REFERENCES

Courtesy, *Conservator of Forests*, Koraput.

Government of India (1976), Dept. of Agriculture & Food Production, National Commission on Agriculture Report at Part IX (Forestry), New Delhi.

Haranath, C.H., "Management of Shifting Cultivation in Orissa" *(Mimeo)*.

Mohapatra, P.C. and S.C. Patnaik, (1982), "Economic of Shifting Cultivation in Koraput District", Prajnan, NIBM, Bombay.

Pati, S.N.; B.K. Patnaik and P.C. Mohapatra (1984), "Shifting Cultivation : A Case Study of Koraput District—Khadi Gramodyog (June), pp. 384-90.

Sharma, R.A., *Shifting Cultivation Dynamics in Orissa (Mimeo)*.

10

ROLE OF FOREST IN A POOR RESOURCE BASE TRIBAL ECONOMY
A Micro Analysis

— *Jagabandhu Samal*

Forests are intimately connected with tribal life, with their multi-dimensional uses. They provide the tribals with food, fodder, fuel, timber, shelter, medicinal drugs, agricultural implements and weapons for hunting. Not only tribal economy but the customs, social fabric and folklore are also shaped and formed by the forests.

The tribals are basically forest dwellers, the original inhabitants in it. They used to get unrestricted rights in getting their requirements in the past. The clearance of forests to meet the increasing demand of rising population, establishment of industrial, mineral and hydro-electricity projects, rehabilitation colonies, to meet industrial and commercial needs, to support ever increasing shifting cultivation and above all, illicit fellings, resulted in a progressive decline in forest growth. The privileges enjoyed by the forest dwellers were restricted and regulated by various forest policies. The principal base of the tribal economy was weakened. Still the existing forest growth plays an important role in the tribal economy.

The Present Study

This chapter is an ecology based economic study of a poor resource region mainly inhabited by the tribals. The study village, Sanabaleswar is one of the samples of four different villages under differing ecological situations, like the hills having some forests cover where the tribals mainly adopt shifting cultivation, the hills which have been completely denuded of forest growth, the situation where tribals adopt settled agriculture and a tribal resettlement colony which was undertaken by the author in undivided Koraput district, for indepth study to prepare the doctoral dissertation. The period of intensive study was a full year, i.e., 365 days, between July 1984 to June 1985.

The Study Village

The study village, Sanabaleswar is a typical tribal village from the 1000 feet plateau region of the undivided Koraput district.[1] It is situated in Gumma Panchayat of Rayagada Block. It is typical in two ways: Firstly, it is situated in the hill region with some forest growth, where shifting cultivation on forest land as well as dependence on forest products for living are quite significant. Secondly, it is typical of the small tribal village with population of around a hundred. As per the 1981 census, 64 per cent of the villages in the 1000 ft. plateau (the present Rayagada district and Narayan Patna P.S. at Koraput district) has a population less than 200 each. If we would add the villages having between 200 and less than 500 population to the above, then 91 per cent of the villages of this plateau has a population less than 500 each. Correspondingly, this plateau had the highest percentage of tribal population (i.e. 65.3) in the villages. (See Table 10.1 for villages classified by population size in different plateaus of undivided Koraput District). Sanabaleswar is an interior tribal village situated at a distance of 12 kms. from Gumma and 25 kms. from Rayagada. A walking path starting from Gumma passes through the village in the hill terrains which is somewhat jeepable in fair weather.

Households and Population

At the time of survey of this village in April 1984, there were 26 households in the village all belonging to 'Kandha' tribe with a total population of 116 of which 56 were males and 60 females. Of this, 15 households were taken in the sample with a population of 74, which included 35 males and 39 females.

Literacy

All but one person, in the village were illiterate. The only literate person a young man, was working as night watchman with a contractor in the nearby mine. He had never gone to school, but while working in the mine, he had, of his own effort learnt a reasonable reading and writing

TABLE 10.1 : Village Classified by Population Size in different Geographical Divisions Based on the Altitudes in Koraput District in 1981 (Undivided)

Sl. No.	Plateaus / Sub-Divn.	No. of inhabited villages	Percentage of villages with size of population						Percentage of tribal rural population
			Less than 200	200-499	500-999	1000-1999	2000-4999	5000 & above	
1.	Koraput sub-division (excluding Narayanpatna P.S. area) (3,000 ft. plateau)	924 (100)	44.10	35.10	14.40	5.20	0.90	0.30	57.80
2.	Jeypore and Nawrangpur sub-divisions (2,000 ft. plateau)	1553	21.20	31.00	28.80	15.40	3.60	—	57.20
3.	Rayagada and Gunupur sub-divisions including Narayanpatna PS. (1,000 ft. plateau)	2679	64.00	26.90	7.30	1.20	0.50	0.10	65.30
4.	Malkangiri sub-division (500 ft. plateau)	701	35.50	35.50	20.10	7.50	1.40	—	62.40
	Total	5857 (100)	46.10	30.30	15.60	6.40	1.30	0.30	60.20

Source : Calculation is based on Census of India, 1981, Series 16, Orissa, Part II-A, pp. 182-85.

in Oriya. Ironically, there was a lower primary school in the village, in the sense that the State government had appointed a teacher for the school, who had almost never showed his face in the village. Of course, there was no school building, nor even possibility of private living quarters for the teacher in the village.

Health and Sanitation

The villagers use the water of a stream for all purposes that flows by the village. The general health condition of the villagers is not good. People, very often, complain of fever, headache, skin diseases and stomach troubles. Once sick, they never prefer to go to a hospital or take advice of a doctor. On the other hand, they try to appease the spirit or gods by performing rituals and sacrificing birds, goats or pigs. The sub-divisional hospital is at Rayagada. Even they do not visit the dispensary at Nishikhal mine area, only at a distance of 4 Kms. from the village.

Working Population

It was estimated that 73 per cent of the total population of the village was in the category of workers, i.e. those who have engaged in gainful activity any time during the year. From among the men 80 per cent, from among women 66.60 per cent, and frcm among the children in the age group 6-14, 70 per cent (38.70 per cent in the age group, 0-14) were found to be employed in gainful activities. All the able bodied persons in the age group 15-59, and 75 per cent of the older people above 60, were working to eke out a living. This was considerably higher than the percentage of the total rural population of the district classified as workers in the 1981 census i.e. 51.10 per cent of which, 50.90 per cent was in the age group 15 to 59 and 13.80, in the age group 0-14. This reflects the situation of the tribals located in this village. For all the adult male workers cultivation was the main activity and collection of minor forest produce (M.F.P.) and food gathering were the subsidiary activities. Similar was the case with half of the working boys. About 30 per cent of the boys spent their time in tending cattle. The situation was different for female workers. For half of them, food gathering was the main activity and for the rest, cultivation, collection of M.F.P. was an important subsidiary activity. In the ecological setting of Sanabaleswar and similar other villages, where there is little land fit for cultivation, gathering food from wooded hills around becomes an important activity of the households, particularly for adult women and girls for living. The sharp difference between the percentage of workers mainly among the adult females and girls in the 1981 census and in our survey, may presumably due to the census ignoring this and forest collection as a productive activity among tribals.

Forest Based Agriculture—"Shifting Cultivation"

The agriculture under Sanabaleswar situation is mainly forest based as the tribals practise shifting cultivation (slash and burn type) locally called "*Podu*".

While defining the shifting cultivation Pelzer[2] outlines the following features :

(1) Rotation of fields, not crops, that is, shifting the fields over time and space, with short period of cropping and long period of fallows :

- (i) use of fire as clearing agent;
- (ii) use of human labour as the chief input;
- (iii) no animal or plough is used for cultivation;
- (iv) use of simple tools like dibble stick or hoe; and
- (v) practice of mixed cropping on the land.

A patch of forest land after it is cleared and the materials burnt, is cultivated for two to three years and then it is left fallow for some years for regeneration. Due to increasing pressure of population and restrictions imposed on forest lands by the government, the cultivation period and the fallow period (shifting cycle) have declined all over. In Sanabaleswar, it has come down to the extent of two to three years.

There were approximately 63 acres of *Podu* land on the hills and 7.60 acres of low dongar land under the Control of the villagers of Sanabaleswar. Naturally, not all *podu* land was put to cultivation every year, but between 40 to 60 per cent of it. Due to steady decline in the *podu* cycle, the quality of land has deteriorated and productivity has gone down to the minimum possible.

Economics of Cultivation

There were 14 cultivating sample households (actually out of the 15 sample households, one family consisting of an old man and old woman did not cultivate its land 0.80 acre independently, instead, joined their

TABLE 10.2 : The Area Sown. Per Acre Yield. Paid Out Cost and Net Farm Income of Crops by the Sample Households in Sanabaleswar during 1984-85

Sl. No.	Name of crops	Area sown (acre)	No. of families sown	No. of families received yield	Per acre yield (Kgs.)	Per acre gross value (Rs.)	Per acre paid out cost (Rs.)	Per acre net farm income (Rs.)
1.	Ragi	5.03	10	10	100.50	106.50	28.25	78.25
2.	Suan	5.74.5	9	7	85.00	63.75	6.75	57.75
3.	Kosla	4.65	11	8	221.50	166.15	5.45	160.07
4.	Kangu	0.32	4	Nil	Nil	Nil	15.60	(–15.60)
5.	Ganthi	0.56	3	3	223.00	334.50	8.70	325.80
6.	Jahna	1.50	9	2	106.50	79.80	5.75	74.10
7.	Jhuranga	0.12.5	1	Nil	Nil	Nil	16.00	(–16.00)
8.	Kandul (Arhar)	0.62	3	1	56.50	225.80	40.00	186.00
9.	Maiza	5.45	8	5	5.30	3.95	4.30	(–0.35)
10.	Alsi (Niger)	8.50	8	7	11.50	46.00	21.00	25.00
	All groups	32.50	14	—	—	79.80	13.70	66.10

son who had a separate households and was included in the sample), who cultivated 32.50 acres of land. All the cultivating sample households had engaged 4,976.50 adult man-days (all types of labour days i.e., adult male, adult female and child labour days converted into adult male days) of labour, most family labour. Hired labour days was only marginal (79 man-days). Exchange labour or labour on the basis of reciprocity was prevalent in the valley.

Table 10.2 shows crop-wise area sown, per acre paid out cost, return and net farm income from agriculture in Sanabaleswar. The sample households have sown 10 different types of crop, mostly mixed. The area figures of land sown had been separately estimated on the basis of proportions of seed sown. Not every crop that was sown was necessarily reaped, some crops even on the same field, failed.

The per acre yield rates for most crops grown were rather poor. How poor, would become clear from the data given in Table 10.3 in which the average yields of crops in Rayagada Sub-divisions, Koraput district and Orissa State along with that of the study village are given.

TABLE 10.3 : Per Acre Yield of Crops in Sanabaleswar and Rayagada Agricultural District (Rayagada Sub-Division) and Orissa State during 1984-85

Sl. No.	*Name of crops*	*Per acre yield in kilogram*			
		Sanabaleswar	*Rayagada sub-divn.*	*Koraput district*	*Orissa State*
1.	Ragi	106.50	326.00	270.00	306.00
2.	Suan	85.00			
3.	Kosla	221.50			
4.	Kangu	nil			
5.	Ganthia	230.00			
6.	All small millets (2 + 3 + 4 + 5)	145.80	202.00	178.00	186.00
7.	Jahna (Jawar)	106.50	445.00	339.00	311.00
8.	Jhuranga	nil	N.A.	121.00	187.00
9.	Kandul (Arhar)	56.50	263.00	242.00	260.00
10.	Maize	5.30	326.00	270.00	222.00
11.	Niger (Alsi)	11.50	161.00	165.00	175.00

Note : For Cols. 4, 5, and 6, data taken from Orissa Agricultural Statistics (1984-85); Directorate of Agriculture and Food Production, Bhubaneswar.

The two immediate causes of crop failure and poor yields in the village during 1984-85 were reported to be drought and depredation by animals. After some heavy showers in July and first-half of August, the rain ceased completely. Secondly, the wild animals like bear, boar, and sambar spoiled crops like kandul, jahna and suans, etc. This, therefore, was partly an abnormal year. But the villagers of Sanabaleswar as well as neighbouring villages said that they were getting yields of this order for four to five consecutive years. This cannot be attributed all to the drought or animals. It is very likely that with shortening of *podu* cycles in the village and in neighbourhood the productivity of land was going down and showing greater sensibility to shortage of rainfall, besides being more exposed to erosion of top soil.

Return from Podu : How Poor Is It?

Agricultural activity engaged people of the village for bulk of the time, but it gave the smallest return per labour day. (See Table 10.4). The earnings per adult male labour day were only 42 paise, which could buy only 420 grams of ragi, (ragi is the common cereal here), the price of ragi being rupee one per one kilogram. Of course, some of the cereals

TABLE 10.4 : Table showing Labour-days Engaged in Gainful Activities, Total Income Received, and Income Received per Man-day in Sanabaleswar during 1984-85

Sl. No.	*Name of the activity*	*Total man-days worked*	*Total income received (Rs.)*	*Income received per man-days (Rs.)*
1.	Own cultivation	4,976 (49.90)	2,096.00 (14.20)	0.42
2.	Agricultural wage labour	147 (1.50)	440.00 (3.00)	3.00
3.	Non-farm work	365 (3.60)	1,105.00 (7.40)	3.04
4.	Livestock work	612 (6.10)	180.00 (1.20)	0.30
5.	Minor forest Produce and firewood collection	1,001 (10.0)	7,229.00 (48.80)	7.22
6.	Food gathering	2,878 (28.90)	3,758.00 (25.40)	1.30
	Total	9,977 (100.00)	14,808.00 (100.00)	1.48

(Figures in the brackets indicate percentage to respective totals)

Note : All labour-days were converted into adult man-days on the basis of : 1 adult male labour day = 1.50 adult female days = 2 child labour days; on the basis of prevailing wage rate of Rs. 3, Rs. 2 and Rs. 1.50 respectively.

produced were less expensive than ragi. If, therefore, we take the total quantity of cereals and pulses (i.e., foodgrains) produced by sample households in their fields, it came to 2,223 Kgs. (This excludes the oil-seed, niger). The production of foodgrains per adult male labour day came to 447 grams only. If we calculate this per consumption unit, it will come only to 90 grams per day per consumption Unit.[3]

Other Gainful Activities

Besides cultivation (i.e., mainly *Podu*), the two other major activities of the households in Sanabaleswar were collection and marketing of M.F.P. and gathering food from the forest. Other gainful activities of less importance were non-farm productive works, livestock work and agriculture wage work.

Agricultural Wage Work

The scope of wage labour, as discussed earlier, was limited. The sample households spent only 1.40 per cent of their gainfully employed days on agricultural wage work (both in and outside the village) and earned 3 per cent of total income (See Table 10.4).

Non-Farm Wage Labour

During the year under study, only one man was engaged as a night watchman in the nearby mines. He worked with a contractor. But mine work was totally stopped. Hence, no other person in the village worked in it during the year. There was no other public works undertaken either in the village or outside.

A minor non-farm work of the self-employment category was illegal distillation and sale of country liquor by a few households. But there was a limit to this activity. Taking total working labour days into account, it was estimated that adult males had spent 5.2 per cent, adult females 2.5 per cent and children 0.2 per cent of their time in such activities. Correspondingly 7.40 per cent of the total income of the sample households was received from this source.

Livestock Activity

The tribals in the village maintain different types of animals and poultry, bullocks, cows, buffalows, pig and poultry. These animals are more in the nature of assets that can be liquidated at will for consumption or given as items of bride price. Only eggs and poultry birds are sometimes sold. The cows and buffalows are not milked. It was estimated that the workers of the sample households had spent 3.6 per cent of total gainfully employed time in watching livestock and received only 1.2 per cent of the income during the year. The per man-day return was only 30 paise. (See Table 10.4).

Collection of Minor Forest Produce

Collection and sale of M.F.P. is usually an important source of employment and income of the tribals. But it depends upon the availability of forest and forest produce in a region inhabited by tribals. The people of Sanabaleswar collect piri (a type of long thatching grass), siali leaves and fibres, karanjia seeds, tamarind and bamboo from nearby forests. A part of the produce is consumed at house and the rest, sold outside. The firewood is mostly consumed at home and sometimes, sold. They extract tamarind seeds, keep seeds to eat, and sell the processed tamarind skin in the *hat*. The most important item of sale is bamboo, which they sell to the basketmakers at Rayagada. It was noticed that on an average, bamboo was cut twice a month between October and April, and once a month, between May and September. Not many people go for cutting bamboo between May and September, whereas in other months people in large number join this operation. It was confessed by the villagers that during May to August, the bamboo culms would generate and grow, and hence, over exploitation was not desirable. Some of the people badly in need of cash do not follow this principle, and go to cut some old pieces during these months.

It was estimated that 384 adult male days, 224 adult women days and only 8 child labour days (in all 537 adult man-days) were spent in cutting and sale of bamboos by the sample households during the period under reference. Correspondingly bamboo worth of Rs. 3,767.00 was extracted during this period. This constituted 52 per cent of the value of total M.F.P. collected (excluding food gathering). Out of the total bamboo cut, 96 per cent was sold and only 4 per cent was used at home by the tribals in the village. It is interesting to note that per adult male day return from collection of bamboo alone comes to Rs. 7 under Sanabaleswar situation. This infact, was the most productive of all activities in which the villagers were engaged.

The cutting of bamboo, carrying by head load to Rayagada during night in order to avoid forest officials, selling it to the basket makers the next day, returning to the village tired, and taking some hours of rest, involved one and half days and one night for each person, each time. Bamboo was sold at the rate of Re. 1.00 per piece at Rayagada. It was noticed that an adult male could carry 15 to 16 pieces, and an adult woman, 10 to 12 pieces of bamboo to the market at a time.

The tribals of Sanabaleswar generally sell other M.F.P. to the private traders at Gumma. In most cases of such sales, they are deprived of the full market price for the product. Under pressing financial needs, they accept advance from the traders who visit weekly *hat* at Gumma. It is agreed at the time of transaction of the loan that it would be repaid in terms of some M.F.P. at a rate agreed at the time. This rate is usually much lower than the expected (and later, actual) market price during the next collection season.

It has been estimated that the working members of the sample households spent 14 per cent of their adult male days, 7 per cent of their adult women days and 4 per cent of their child labour days, out of the total gainfully employed days of the year, in collection of M.F.P. including firewood. On the other hand, they received 35 per cent of their total income from the sale value (48.80 per cent of total income when we add to it 13.8 per cent to the value consumed) of M.F.P., in which sale of bamboo has the major share. The firewood which they collect is used not only for cooking the meal, but also to keep the fire burning throughout the night to save them from cold during winter and also to keep wild animals away. It was found during our field investigation that 9 out of 15 sample households (i.e., 60 per cent) did not buy kerosene oil any day to light their houses, as they expressed their inability to buy the same. They take their dinner early, and sleep near the fire place in a circle. All these show the important role that forest products plays in the economy of tribals in the type of tribal setting characterised by Sanabaleswar.

Food Gathering

As the return from agriculture is insufficient to meet the food needs of the tribals, they supplement it with food gathering from hills and forests. They generally collect various edible roots, fruits, and leaves. Occasionally, they go for hunting. The major item in collected food under Sanabaleswar situation is various kinds of root (*Kanda*) dug out of ground. They also collect leaves of some trees (*Saga*) and seasonal fruits like mango, jack fruits, dimbiri fruit, and adangaphal to eat.

Mango stones and tamarind seeds are powdered and then made into gruel with other food items like ragi, suan or kosla, etc. for consumption.

Role of Women and Children in Food Gathering

In the collection and gathering of food, women and children spend major part of their working time; male members put in only a little work. Our survey showed that adult women spent 51 per cent and children 32 per cent of their total gainfully occupied labour days in digging roots and collecting other food articles. Adult males had spent only 15.5 per cent of their time in it. It was estimated that 25 per cent of total family income of the sample households was derived from food gathering.

Labour Employment in Various Tasks—A Comparative Analysis

It may be useful to know, what proportion of their total time the villagers spent on these gainful activities and which activities kept the workers engaged for what part of the time. It would be interesting to notice the time the villagers spent in unproductive tasks. The relevant data are presented in Table 10.5. These are based on the information on daily time disposition of every member during 365 days, between 1st July, 1984 and 30th June, 1985.

The data show that adult males spent 72 per cent of the time in gainful activities, out of which 47 per cent was on farm work, almost all of it on work on own farms. The other two important productive works on which tribals spent time were collection of M.F.P. and firewood and food gathering which claimed 10 and 11 per cent of the time respectively. 28 per cent of the time, they were apparently outside labour force, in the sense that they were either engaged in domestic works or in festivity or were unwell.

The pattern of time disposition was somewhat different for women and children. Adult women spent 62 per cent of their time in gainful works; the bulk of which i.e., over 35 per cent, in food gathering and collection of M.F.P. Agriculture occupied about 25 per cent of the time. Naturally domestic works and festivities, etc., kept them busy for 38 per cent of time during the year.

Excepting the three children who were fully busy in looking after livestock, the bulk of other children's time was spent mainly in food gathering and to a lesser extent in farm work.

TABLE 10.5 : Percentage Distribution of 365 days of 21 Adult Males, 21 Adult Females and 13 Child Workers in Sanabaleswar from July 1984 to June 1985

Sl. No.	*Name of the task*	*Percentage of labour days spent*		
		Adult male	*Adult female*	*Child workers*
1.	Work on own farm	45.50	24.00	14.00
2.	Wage work on others' farm	1.50	0.70	—
3.	Livestock work	0.40	—	24.50
4.	Non-farm productive work	3.70	1.60	0.20
	Total 1 to 4	51.10	26.30	38.70
5.	Collection of MFP & firewood	9.90	3.80	2.50
6.	Food gathering	11.20	31.60	19.50
	Total of 5 and 6 (forest collection)	21.10	35.40	22.00
	Total 1 to 6 (productive works)	72.20	61.70	60.70
7.	Repair and maintenance of own houses	0.30	0.10	0.10
8.	Purely domestic work	17.40	31.40	35.00
9.	Festivity	3.90	3.80	2.70
10.	Visits to relations	0.50	0.30	0.30
11.	Marketing day	1.80	1.50	0.50
12.	Sick	3.90	1.20	0.70
	Total 7-12 (Unproductive work)	27.80	38.30	39.30
	Grand total of 1 to 12	100.0	100.00	100.00

When these tribal workers were not engaged in whatever gainful activity they can engage themselves in, they usually spent time at home and when asked, reported that they were doing domestic work. It does not mean that, if they found that there was some productive work available, they would not engaged themselves in it.

Return from Gainful Activities—The Importance of Forest Collection and Gathering

For all the labour that these tribal villagers applied to the forest land (*Podu* or otherwise—all illegal exploitation), how much did they earn? Table 10.4 gives the relevant data. It would be found from the table that the workers of Sanabaleswar, on an average, earned Rs. 1.48 per day of work of an adult male labour. This was just about half the prevailing daily wage rate of hired agricultural labour (i.e., Rs. 3) prevalent in the locality during the year. This amount of total income of an adult male, could buy 1.500 Kgs. of ragi, if we convert it into ragi, the most stable food of the tribals.

Agriculture *versus* Forest Collection

Although the villagers spent half of their gainfully employed time in agriculture in *Podu* they received only 14.2 per cent of their total income. It was merely 42 paise per man-day of work.

On the other hand, two important sources of employment and income, other than cultivation, are food gathering and collection of minor forest produce including firewood and bamboo. Food gathering from hills and forests, mainly by women and children, and also partly by men, occupied 29 per cent of total man-days of work and yielded a quarter (25.4 per cent) of total income. This gives an average of Rs. 1.30 a man day. Food gathered from the forest is all consumed. The value of food gathering was more than three times that in agriculture.

Forest collection including bamboo and firewood occupied only one-tenth of their total man-days of effort, but produced almost half (48.8 per cent) of total income. The average productivity per man-day of work was Rs. 7.22, almost two and a quarter times the daily agricultural wage rate in the village, and even higher than the highest wage rate in farming even in settled agriculture in the district (Rs. 6) despite the fact that some of the M.F.P. had to be sold by the villagers to traders at considerably lower than the market price. In effect, bamboo stolen from the forest and sold, sustained the tribal households for half the year.

Other gainful activities like agricultural wage work, livestock work, and non-farm work, as discussed earlier, were of minor importance.

Income from Gainful Activities—How Poor It Is?

It was estimated that the total income from all gainful activities of the sample households during the year was Rs. 14,808.00. Based on this, the annual per household income came to Rs. 987.00 and per capita, Rs. 200.00.

The Ministry of Rural Development, Government of India, in order to select the poorest households to be eligible for I.R.D.P. benefits kept the yardstick of Rs. 3,500 per family or Rs. 700 per capita (with 1979-80 base prices). A family or individual not able to earn this income would be treated as poor. This yardstick was for Sixth plan. Our data related to the last year of the Sixth Plan, i.e., 1984-85. By this measure, even unadjusted for the rise in price level since 1979-80, the average level of living was much below the poverty line. If we adjust it to the base year price of 1979-80, the annual per household income would come to Rs. 710.80 and per capita Rs. 144. This shows the miserable economic position of the tribals living under Sanabaleswar condition, inspite of the fact that most tribal men and women, and a large proportion of children are engaged in gainful activities for a large number of days of the year.

Approach to Development and Policy Implications

How can the economic condition of these tribals improve? The economy of Sanabaleswar (Sanabaleswar is a representative village of micro tribal villages in 1000 feet plateau where *Podu* cultivation is the main type of agriculture) shows that while shifting cultivation yields a very low return, the tribal households get almost half their annual income by illegally harvesting a headload of bamboo once every fortnight in the surrounding forest. This clearly indicates that bamboo is a much better source of income than any agricultural product on this hill and forest land.

Economics of Bamboo Cultivation

An acre of land can sustain 500 clumps of bamboos (Ram Prakash and Khanna : 1979, Ch. 13) at a distance of 4 mts. × 4 mts., and from the fourth year onwards can yield a steady stream of 6 bamboos per clump for harvesting after retaining about 6 bamboos to give support to new ones, giving about 3000 bamboos per year. In the village like Sanabaleswar the *Podu* land can be converted into bamboo plantations with much better results than agriculture on it. The households of Sanabaleswar have 63 acres of *podu* land under their possession. Besides they were regularly stealing bamboo from the neighbouring forest area. If every household can, somehow, have 3 to 5 acres of such land for bamboo plantation, each household can obtain 8 to 12 thousand bamboos per year from the fourth year onwards. Since a bamboo can sell at an average price of Rs. 1.50, the gross receipts would vary from Rs. 12,000 to Rs. 18,000 a year, or Rs. 1,000 to Rs. 15,000 a month.

But there are three problems associated with this : (a) where to get land from, (b) the know-how about planting, and (c) the ability of tribal households to sustain itself for 3-4 years before the first lot of bamboos can be harvested. Let us find out the possible ways :

(a) The podu land as well as the land on which bamboo grows, belong to the State under the control of the Forest Department or Revenue Department. These Departments are not in a position to prevent *Podu* cultivation totally. If tribals are allotted 3 to 5 acres of land per family under usufructuary inheritable lease for sylvicultural use only, the forest cover of the land can be increased, the economic condition of tribals would improve, and the remainder of the forest area would be spared from unsystematic exploitation.

Social Forestry Project

The Orissa State Government's Social Forestry Project provides for such plantations under its scheme. The two main plantation activities which are envisaged under the project include : (i) Establishment of community plantations, and (ii) establishment of private plantations. The community plantation is undertaken on Government Waste lands, barren hills, village common land, etc., from which the villagers with permit from the Village Forest Committee (V.F.C.) can extract the produce. The private plantations include : (a) farm forestry on private land, land unfit for agriculture, orchard lands, backyards of residential houses and along field bunds, and (b) forest farming for Rural Poor (F.F.R.P.). The latter aims at helping the landless families including tribals, to practise agro-forestry or intensive forestry on marginal government land in and around the village. (Patnaik, *et al.*, 1989). Under F.F.R.P. scheme the State Government proposes to allot 0.50 hectare of land (1.23 acres) to every landless or tribal household. All the beneficiaries in a village will be allotted land in contiguous blocks for better watch and ward and economy in maintenance cost. The State will provide seedlings, fertilisers, pesticides and wage for field operation, planting and other operations in order to establish the plantations for first-three years. This is the "Tree-Patta" scheme where beneficiaries will have right on plantation but not on the land.

This F.F.R.P. scheme appears well suited to tribal villages like Sanabaleswar, except that the scheme visualises giving only 0.50 hectares of land to every household. The tribal households should be permitted a little more of forest land than what they illegally use to-day for *Podu*, in order to make an effective start in sylviculture (i.e., at least about 2 hectares per family). It is important to note that inadequate land resource to households in such schemes can, in the end, only frustrate every one including the Government and end in failure, as the case of resettlement schemes of the tribals.

The plantation in all the 2 hectares of land should not be done at a stretch, but in annual stages. Apart from obviating the shortage of labour for plantation, it will stagger availability of wage employment to tribal households on their own leased lands over a period of 4 years. The stoppage of '*Podu*' cultivation on such lands will not be total in the very first year, but in annual stages.

(b) The tribals cannot just be left to the planting for themselves, even if the seedlings, etc. are provided free. It is necessary to remember that while the tribal lives in the forest, through pre-history and history, he is familiar with harvesting properly the forest produce, but not planting tree, which for him just naturally generates. The forest guards of the area can be converted into extension workers on forestry for tribals and guide them in plantation and preservation works.

(c) While staggering plantations will ensure some money wages to the tribal households every year for at least four years until the first harvest is due, and the elemination of *Podu* cultivation in similar annual stages, will help the tribal households to obtain part of subsistence every year, this will by itself be inadequate for the purpose. Unless alternative wage opportunities are provided to him the whole scheme runs the risk of failing. Therefore, the State must organise public works like road construction, provision of perennial protected drinking and household water supply devices on nearby streams, watershed schemes for irrigation, and other works for at least 3 to 4 years in the neighbourhood of the village. Fortunately there are enough such work opportunities in the 1000 feet plateau type tribal lands.

In this proposal for plantations, the emphasis, so far, has been put on bamboos. The other trees that can be mentioned are fuel wood trees. Horticultural trees which are productive and economically sustainable in this region should be welcome, it is necessary to start with trees, whose marketing would be the easiest and which will provide a steady income after 3 or 4 years of waiting time. Bamboo and certain other fuelwood trees fill this gap.

Land Colonisation Scheme as an Alternative

The land colonisation scheme was devised to wean the tribals and others away from shifting cultivation to new settlements in the plateau and plains where the households were given land for cultivation and houses to live in. The settlers were provided with agricultural implements including bullocks and seeds. Other facilities in the colony included communication, drinking water, school building and shop for essential commodities.

The land colonisation scheme in Orissa was formulated by the Harijan and Tribal Welfare Department in the First Plan period. Some of the colonies were also started by the Forest Department during the same period. Out of the 95 such colonies were established by the Harijan and Tribal Welfare Department, 29 colonies were established in undivided Koraput district during First and Second Plan period. Another colony was later established for Bonda tribals at Mudulipada. A total number of 968 families had been brought to these colonies.

But various evaluation reports show that the scheme has failed to achieve its objective properly. There has been large scale desertion of the settlers from the colonies. The Annual Administrative Report of the T & R.W. Department, Government of Orissa, for 1963-64 states, "In course of time it was noticed that either the settlers were reluctant to live in the new colonies divorced from their old neighbours or it was not possible to provide all necessary amenities in the colonies as a result of ceiling in expenditure. In any case, the colonies hardly proved attractive. During the Third Plan, therefore, no new colonies were started. . . . The Government shops were closed down as they did not function properly". It has been pointed out by the Shilu A.O. Committee that, "the basic weakness in many of these programmes lies in the assumption of the planners that with the grant of land, provision of houses and supply of bullocks, enough has been done to enable a tribal to earn a living. What is not recognised is that building up of fertility of virgin land takes time and that its productivity after reclamation is not always enough to maintain a tribal family".[4]

Our indepth study of an old Adibasi colony in the 1000 ft. plateau, in the undivided Koraput district revealed that :

(a) 32 families, all belonging to Kandha tribe, were brought from 10 different villages and settled in the Bamsadhara valley near Kumbharadhamuni village under Bissamcuttack Block. By the time the survey was undertaken (1984-85), it was found that 18 original settlers' families (56 per cent) had already deserted.

(b) But at the time of field investigation there were 24 families in the colony, which constituted.

(1) 14 of the original setlers, (2) 5 extended families of these 14 families, as the boys after marriage preferred to stay separate, (3) 5 families had immigrated to the colony afterwards.

(c) It was found that 75 per cent of the settled land (96 acres) provided for cultivation was left fallow, even though about 50 per cent of the colony land was irrigated by the canal flowing from the small dam made for the purpose. The settlers complained that the land supplied to them in this patch was very poor in quality i.e., "Kharimati", or saline land. No effort had yet been made by any agency to treat this land and improve its quality.

(d) On the other hand, the settlers of the colony went for agricultural wage labour which was available in the paddy lands of non-tribal big landlords of main Kumbhardhamuni village and in the neighbouring villages.

(c) While the bulk of their paddy land remained uncultivated, 17 households had made incursion into the forest area of the nearby hills and brought some land under shifting cultivation. These tribals are accustomed to *Podu* cultivation. But that is not the main cause of their going for shifting cultivation. The main reason is that, bulk of the operations in *Podu* fields are done when there is less or no work in settled paddy fields, and hence demand for agricultural wage labour is less. The tribal labourers will give up this little *Podu* (12.85 acres), if wage labour is available in the off season.

The tribals can be weaned away from *Podu* cultivation by being given adequate good·quality land for cultivation with irrigation facility, with provision for Rabi season, or in the absence of it, continuous wage employment in public and private works particularly during winter and summer months.

REFERENCES

1. Since 1992, the Koraput district has been divided into four parts, each being a district, i.e., (i) Koraput (consisting of Koraput Sadar and Jeypore Subdivisions), (ii) Nawrangpur, (iii) Malkangiri and (iv) Rayagada (consisting of Rayagada and Gunupur sub-divisions).
2. Pelzer, K.J., *Pioneer Settlement in Asiatic Topic*, Clark and Haswall (1954), p. 33.
3. Consumption Units have been calculated by taking adult male as 1, adult female as 0.75 and children below 14 years as 0.4. While the conversion Units for adult

male and adult female are as per ICMR conversion rates, for children it is an average of detailed rates for different age groups of children. For details refer to "Recommended Dietary Intake for Indians", Indian Council of Medical Research Ansary Nagar, New Delhi (1981).

4. *Government of India : Planning Commission (1969).* All India Committee on Plan Projects "Report of the Study Team on Tribal Development Programmes", New Delhi (mimeo), pp. 31.

REFERENCES

Bell, R.C.S. (1945), *Orissa District Gazetteers, Koraput,* Cuttack, Govt. of Orissa Press.

Bose, Saradindu (1972), "Problems of Shifting Cultivation in India" in M.L. Patel (ed). *Agro-Economic Problems of Tribal India, Bhopal,* Progress Publishers.

Dhar, Usha (1970), "Shifting Cultivation in Hill Tracts of India", *I.J.A.E.*, Vol. XXV, July-Sept., No. 3.

Fernandes, W. and Geeta Memon (1987), *Tribal Women and Forest Economy—Deforestation, Exploitation and Status Change*, New Delhi : Indian Social Institute.

Mohapatra, P.C. and D. Panda (ed.) (1978), *Tribal Problems of Today and Tomorrow,* Bhubaneswar, Sabari Cultural Society.

Mohapatra, P.C. (1987), *Economic Development of Tribal India*, New Delhi, Ashis Publishing House.

Mishra, Baniprasanna (1970), *Problems of Socio-Economic Adjustment of Tripura Jhumias*, Poona (G.I.P.E.), Doctoral Dessertation.

Patnaik, L.K. *et al.*, (ed) (1989), *Social Forestry Hand Book for Orissa*, Bhubaneswar, SIDA.

Pelzer, K.J. (1954), *Pioneer Settlement in Asiatic Tropic*, Clark and Haswell.

Patel, M.L. (ed) (1972), *Agro-Economic Problems of Tribal India*, Bhopal, Progress Publishers.

Rao, P.S.B. (ed) (1985), *Tribal and Forest Eco-System*, Koraput, D.V.A. College.

Ram Prakash and L.S. Khanna (1979), *The Theory and Practice of Sylvicultural System*, New Delhi, Periodical Expert Book Agency.

Samal, J. (1979), *Problems of Tribal Agriculture in India*, Poona, M.Phil. Dissertation, University of Poona, (G.I.P.E.).

Samal, J. (1992), *Some Aspects of Tribal Economy—A Case Study of Koraput District*, Poona, Doctoral Dissertation, University of Poona, (G.I.P.E.).

Saha, N. (1970), *The Economics of Shifting Cultivation in Assam*, Assam, Doctoral Dissertation, Gauhati University.

Shah, Tushar (1988), *Gains from Social Forestry, Lesson from West Bengal*, Sussex, Institute of Development Studies.

Tripathy, D.P. (1952), *Shifting Cultivation in Orissa—Its Cause, Effects and Remedy*, Cuttack, Orissa Govt. Press.

Wadia, F.K. (1976), "Control of Shifting Cultivation in North-East India" *Prajnan*, Vol. V, No. 3, July-September.

11

A LOOK AT TRIBALS AND FOREST

— *S.P. Gantayat*

The life of tribals always centred around the forests. The religious, cultural and economic activities of the tribal people depend on forests. Forest is their main life supporting system, and therefore, it plays a vital role in their economy. At the same time the tribal people also know how to use the forest resources rationally and preserve it for posterity. The relationship between forests and tribals is a symbiotic one. In fact, the relationship was perfect and harmonious till few decades back. Since last three to four decades this relationship is fast changing to the disadvantage of both. This is mainly due to interference of outside agencies including government to exploit forest wealth in the name of tribal development. It is noticed that, all developmental activities in the tribal areas have little impact on tribal communities.

Koraput district in Orissa is a glaring example where number of developmental projects have come up involving thousands of crores of rupees. These projects include big industries like H.A.L. at Sunabeda, Alumina plant at Damanjodi, paper mills at Rayagada and Jeypore, Ferrosilicon plant at Therubali, major hydro-electricity and irrigation projects like Kolab, Machkund, Balimela, many small scale industries, railway projects etc. Inspite of all these developmental projects, the local tribal population remains as backward as they were decades back. Certain specific tribal development projects are operating in the district both by government and voluntary agencies since pretty long time. Even after spending hundreds of crores of rupees in the name of development of tribals, no perceptible change is found in the socio-economic life of these people. The only visible and perceptible thing is the exploitation of tribals by outside contractors, industrialists in collusion with forest and revenue officials. The dominant commercial and industrial forces are continuously exploiting the forest wealth. As a result, forests are destroyed to a great extent to the disadvantage of tribals. On the other hand government includes more forest area under reserved category in order to protect forests, thus reducing the forest land for *podu* cultivation and collection of minor forest produce by tribals. Naturally, tribals feel squeezed between the unfavourable forces. Of course, government sometimes allows certain limited facilities in the protected forest for the tribals who always feel that the forest is their homeland. The situation is much like entering in somebody's house and after grabbing everything, offer very little to rightful owner as concession as if showing mercy. The question arises, who is the owner of the forest? Whose property is it? To the tribals, the forest was the property of the community which had to be preserved according to need and for posterity. Government always views forest as a source of revenue only. Industrialists always consider forests as source of raw materials. Thus forests which is an integral part of tribal system, is viewed only as a source of revenue or raw materials. This tendency developed due to commercial exploitation of forests. These forests were the life-line of the tribals till recently. In the name of protection, they lost all rights on forest, what was rightfully theirs. The tribals, faced with ever-increasing shortages of food, fuel, fodder and raw materials, are forced into the status of menial labour. The outside contractors, businessmen, industrialists use these backward population as cheap labour and their natural resources as cheap raw material. The backwardness of the local tribal people is due to their non-integration in the prevailing economic activity or integration only as cheap labour, often bonded and hence exploited. Koraput is a rich district with full of natural resources. Many of these natural resources are being continuously exploited by the government and outside agencies at the cost of the local tribal people.

There are several natural and man-made factors which contribute to the destruction of forests. The natural causes are floods, droughts, parasites (climbers), wild-animals, termites, fire and accidents. The man made causes are planned development (i.e. construction of projects like railway lines, roads, dams, canals and industrial plants and rehabilitation projects), use of timber, other forest produce for raw material. In the second category, tribals or forest dwellers also cause deforestation by cutting trees for fuel, *podu* cultivation, fencing and house construction. The destruction in this case is to a limited extent. But the recent trend is to sell fire wood, charcoals and bamboo by the tribals in the nearby towns for survival. The greatest damage is done to the forests by illegal felling by contractors in connivance with officials, and in a few cases by powerful political leaders.

The result of all these, is massive and large scale deforestation which has reached to an alarming proportion and the present forest coverage is far less than the required 33 per cent for a sound ecology. The recommended requirement of forest cover for mountainous regions is 60 per cent whereas the actual forest coverage is even less than 20 per cent. This is very much evident in the Koraput region where the hills have been denuded and barren. Large scale deforestation leads to ecological imbalance, non-availability of forest produce and non-availability of raw material for forest based industries. It also influences the rainfall, atmospheric quality and causes floods, landslides, soil erosion and other natural disasters. The ultimate victims are the tribals.

What is wrong in the developmental schemes launched by the government for the tribals? The basic defect in such schemes is that, they are planned centrally without taking into consideration the ground realities existing in the different remote pockets. A particular scheme may be suitable in one area and may not be suitable in other areas as there are differences in ecological situations. When such a centrally planned scheme is experimented unsuccessfully the result is wastage of money and manpower and resultant frustrations. The bureaucrats are only after achieving the target and they have no time to see or analyse how successful the scheme is for tribal upliftment. In the process the developmental funds are siphoned off in wrong channels or the right channels are porous. The most important thing is to see the local conditions, needs and the existing skills of the beneficiaries at the time of implementation of a scheme. In other words, the suitability of a scheme for a particular area should be determined first. It must be remembered that the forests and tribals are just like two sides of a coin. The allround development of tribals depends on forests and vice versa. Therefore, the utmost importance should be given to preservation of forests and creation of new forests to compensate the loss of green cover in the last few decades. Massive afforestation and reforestation programmes should be taken up effectively. In these programmes the association of local people is very much essential and the plant species should be chosen very carefully taking into consideration the local conditions. Tribals all along used to get most of their necessities from the forests. The forests have come up naturally. They never know the technique and care of raising different plant species. They have been exploiting the forests since time immemorial. Therefore, necessary training should be imparted to them in this respect by forest extension workers in the village level. In tribal areas, the villages are usually very small. Sometimes a village consists of only 10 to 15 houses. In such cases a group of villages should be taken together and the centrally located village should be taken as the key or model village. The village level extension workers in the fields of forest, health care, education etc. can easily operate from this model village to implement the viable schemes in the government.

Though these Adivasi people have practically no formal education, they do not lack the power of understanding. They can very well judge what is good for them. Once these people are convinced, then the desired result will come automatically without much effort. The creation of village forests in the vicinity of the villages be given top priority. This will cater to the needs of the villagers and ease out pressure on the protected or reserved forests. Once these tribals are actively involved as partners in the creation of village forests, then they will take care of protecting and using the same properly. The question comes how to create a patch of natural forest in the vicinity of a village. The social forestry department instead of taking up plantation of few quick growing species on the road sides and vacant lands, should better concentrate on raising village forest involving the villagers. The average population of tribal villages in the Koraput region ranges between 100 to 250. If a forest is developed with plant species belonging to fibre, fruit, fodder, fuel, timber and other minor forest products yielding varieties in a 5 hectares area of land near a village, it will sustain to the needs of the villagers. The availability of a patch of 5 hectares of vacant forest or revenue land nearby the villages is not at all difficult at least in Koraput district. Forest department has to take care with the help of villagers initially for a period of three years. After that villagers will take care of the whole thing with little guidance from forest department people. This forest will be the community property of the villagers. Community culture is very much in existence among the tribal people. Only a bit of encouragement in this respect will suffice and the tribal people will certainly manage and maintain the village forests. They can easily procure their basic needs from the village forest and distribute among themselves. This will have a double advantage for both government and tribal people. The reserved and protected forests will be saved and new forests will come up with active involvement of tribals who will also come to know about the techniques of plantation.

This patch of forest (i.e. the village forest) should have a outer ring with *Agave americana, Duranta plumeri* etc. as fencing plants which will give very good protection to the forest in the formative years from grazing animals. The plantation of slow growing timber yielding species like sisal, teak, sal, sirish etc. has to be taken up in the central core region. Outer to this core, perennial fruit bearing trees like mango, jack fruit, tamarind, jamun, aonla etc. should be planted. The next layer has to be developed with patches of quick growing species like Acacia. Cassia, Eucalyptus, including Bamboo. In the outermost ring close to the fencing, plants like papaya, guava, custard apple etc. can be grown easily. In this way if a forest can be raised, the villagers will certainly turn into a happy lot and each one of them will be no less than a forest guard without uniform to protect the forest. So, a sort of sustainable natural forest can be raised in the vicinity of villages instead of monoculture plantations carried out by social forestry department here and there spending a lot of money. In most of these social forest plantations, the mortality rate is very high, growth slow and plants start disappearing from the third year. All this happens due to lack of a sense of involvement among local people. The sense of involvement and belongingness can be inculcated in the minds of tribals in the efforts of creating village forests for them.

12

JOINT FOREST MANAGEMENT IN TRIBAL AREAS
Conflicts and Resolutions

— *Achyut Das*

Joint Forest Management (JFM)

There is an air of seriousness regarding the Joint Forest Management (JFM) in the country. From Gujarat to West Bengal and from Himachal Pradesh to Tamil Nadu every State is talking about it, passing various Government Resolutions and taking policy decisions. Orissa is not far behind in the entire exercise. The documents available from different States on JFM offer a very interesting reading. Every State has its Village Forest Protection Committee. We can give a summary of the JFM adopted in different States as follows:

Status of Joint Forest Management

Name of the State	*Status of Joint Forest Management*	*Management at the Village/Panchayat level*
Gujarat	Empowered by Govt. Resolutions	Formation of Forest Protection Committee
Haryana	Empowered by Resolutions of Haryana Forest Department	Hill Resources Management Unit
Uttar Pradesh	Empowered by Govt. Resolutions	Van Panchayat
West Bengal	Empowered by Govt. Resolutions	Van-O-Bhumi Sanskar Sthai Samiti

(*Contd.*)

Name of the State	*Status of Joint Forest Management*	*Management at the Village/Panchayat level*
Orissa	Empowered by Govt. Resolutions	Vana Samrakshyana Samiti
Himachal Pradesh	Empowered by Govt. Resolutions	Village Cooperative Forest Society

This author has extensively travelled in the tribal areas and assessed the implications of Joint Forest Management in practice from Mayurbhanj to Malkangiri and from Gandhamardhan Hills of Sambalpur district to Mahendragiri of Gajapati district. The tribals in general feel that the concept of Joint Forest Management is quite relevant to their socio-economic and cultural environment but question the operational viability. The questions that comes to their mind are:

Relation between Tribals and Local Forest Officials

- What is the guarantee that the non-tribals, often in connivance with the local forest officials, cut the trees?
- Is there any bias in support of the tribals regarding the formation of the Van Samrakshyan Samities?
- How serious is the expectations that in the task of regeneration and restoration of degraded forest, Forest Department and the tribals will be equally partners?
- Who will decide the Joint Forest Management Plan?
- Regarding the usufructory benefit, whether the members of Van Samrakshyan Samiti will have any real benefit?
- Why is there only questions of "Wage" involved in price of Minor Forest Produce collected by the tribals associated with Van Samrakshyan Samiti?
- Though the Forest Department talks about decentralised management under Joint Forest Management structure, why is there so much control by the Forest Department?

Concept and Practice of Joint Forest Management

Analysing the entire concept and practice of Joint Fore[illegible]nt, I have to c[illegible] visualise certain conflicts. These [illegible] can have resolutions through consultation and operational framework among the tribals, Forest officials, the policy-makers and the Non-Governmental Organisations. Conflict arise out of existing frame-work in the forest department and resolutions are possible by a shift of emphasis. Let us list the conflicts as follows:

Conflict I: Between State Priorities and Local Needs

It is clearly seen that the tribals are very severely affected by poverty, malnutrition, lack of food security, fuel wood scarcity, fodder scarcity. Hence, there is always pressure on the forest to get more food, fuel wood, fodder and fibre from the forest. On the other hand, the State Government is aware of maintaining certain minimum area under forest cover to fulfil ecological and environmental needs. Sanctuaries and National parks, Bio-spheres reserves and Game reserves demand more forest areas at the cost of the tribals. There is also a conflict between the policy and practice. Tribals are stopped from using the forest but industrialisation is destroying forest with Government consent.

Conflict II: Between Management of Common Property Resources and Concerns of Earning Daily Bread

Tribals and Forest Dwellers are always concerned about earning their daily bread/minimum subsistence from the forest. They go for *Podu*/ shifting cultivation by destroying the forest. They also try to collect the seasonal Minor Forest Produce. This is the crux of this tribal economy. However, the environmental cost of this practices are heavy. At times they are not aware of the scientific management of common property resources. Gandhi has rightly said that for a poor man food is God. Driven by pangs of hunger, the poor tribal is compelled per force to look into his immediate need rather than long-term benefits. In absence of the alternatives, *Podu* has become a way of life.

Conflict III: Between Supply of Firewood and Demand

In tribal areas of Koraput and many other tribal pockets the supply of fuel wood is becoming a scarce. For generation they have been traditionally using fuelwood freely. Now they are feeling hardship in terms of directly and indirectly paying for it and at times walking miles. The tribal women are the worst sufferers. The demand for fuelwood has increased with rising population and changing of lifestyle.

Conflict IV: Between Forest Managers and Tribals

Forest is differently perceived by different categories of people. Tribals and Forest Dwellers see the forest as their economic base and the life and death of their entire socio-cultural ethos. The local users of the forest resources visualise the forest as a source of different raw materials and plan for its commercial and industrial use. The Forest Managers think that forest is their domain of power and control. The conflict arise out of diverse interest and at times create an obstacle to establish a sound and workable system of management. If Forest Managers emphasise pure forestry, the tribals support a system of Agro-forestry.

Conflict V: Conflict within Forest Administration

If the conflicts between Forest Managers and the local users is one dimension, the other dimension is the internal conflicts within the forest departments. One school of thought concentrates on participatory management of the forest. By understanding the local hopes and aspirations, it depicts their conscious efforts to consult people and develop a people oriented afforestation programme. They believe that the concept of traditional forestry has become obsolete and forestry for people's development is to be planned and implemented. However, the others strong school of thought is to attempt to prevent any kind of interference of the local people particularly tribals in the management and conservation of forest areas. The policy makers are always caught in this conflict situation. Another example of conflict is the plantation policy. One group of Forest Managers think of commercial and industrial plantation and resort to mono-cropping. The other group of Forest Managers think in terms of plantation relevant to the people and to the agro-climatic conditions and believe in the concept of agro-forestry.

Conflict VI: Between Investment Policy and Utilisation Policy for Revenue

It is often seen that forest resources are taken by the State as a resource for raising the revenue and there is always thought of commercial exploitation. Forest Development Corporations in so many names after oriented themselves to raise their revenue. It is noticed that plantations undertaken by Forest Departments has a poor investment policy. Nobody bothers about how much would be required to initiate, maintain and sustain forestry programmes. There is a wide gap between the State

Perspective and the Tribal Perspective. The forestry programmes are often aided by bilateral and multi-lateral agencies and there is not adequate focus in these programmes. The rate of deforestation seems to be high. With the reasons already known and understood even then there is no priority investment policy and long-term planning to reverse this trend.

Conflict VII: Between Price and Wage

The collection of Minor Forest Produce plays a dominant role in the tribal economy. However, this process of collection, procurement, marketing and processing is not always controlled by the tribals. The policy of nationalisation and increasing monopolies given to certain industrial houses, results in giving certain wage to the tribals though the price attached to the Minor Forest Produce is different issue altogether. The "Wage" is exploitative in the tribal areas and the "price" is non-remunerative. The State control is absolute and without an ideological frame-work the tribals are just the part time workers and wage earners in the entire economies of forest.

Participation as Ways and Means of Conflict Resolution

If the forest is to survive and the deforestation is to be arrested, there has to be a workable and participatory mode of management at the grass-root level. There has to be consciousness resolutions by synthesizing conservation strategies development priorities and tribals need, the forest can be protected, regenerated and conserved. Every player in the game (people, Forest Managers, local users, policy-makers) have to work as a team and build up a mutual trust and confidence in one another. Right from the planning stage to the harvesting, the forest issue is to be treated as the issue of all concerned alone confined alone to the State Forest Department. Examples which are readily available show that with motivation and mutual trust, the local population have come forward to protect their own forest and a sense of belonging has been exhibited. Government is increasingly creating an institutional structure to facilitate people's involvement at various levels. Our Van Samarakshyan Samiti is one such concept in practice. The present concept of management of forest is based on scientific and technological principles. It is also a fact that local people and the forest dwellers and the tribal have their own system of sustainable forest management. The guiding principle should, therefore, always be the indigenous principles of co-existence—between man and nature. The so called modern forestry management techniques are to be demystified. In the ultimate sense the management plan of a forest is not only the management plan for trees and plants, flora and fauna, eco-system and environment but essentially it is the management plan for the tribals and the forest dwellers. In essence, there lies the stake for survival of both. Is it not?

To Strengthen People's Management of Forest

To strengthen people's management of forest, what is required is the awareness—social, economic, political, environment—and the skills. Awareness can come with the involvement whereas the skills can be given by imparting training through Forest Department.

13

TRIBAL WOMEN AND FOREST ECONOMY

— *B.B. Mishra*

Indian society is one of the most inegalitarian society. The bases of disparities are mainly caste, sex, ethnicity and place of residence. There are layers and layers of disparities between males and females, between people living in remote areas and urban areas, between economically less advanced and more advanced regions. The most deprived section of all is the Scheduled Tribe female living in rural areas of backward region. After the attainment of independence, India committed itself to achieve an egalitarian social order. As per Article 46 of the Directive Principles of State Policy, the State was directed to "promote with special care the education and economic interests of the weaker sections of the society, and in particular of scheduled castes, scheduled tribes and girls". Planned efforts have been made since independence and as a result the situation of the backward regions and deprived groups has improved but not to the expected level. The process of modernisation has done little to improve the status of women in general and of Tribal female in particular. As remarked by Raza and Premi "The process of modernisation in these societies has followed a pattern of creating dual economy—one with capital intensive modern sector, the other with labour intensive traditional stereotyped colonialism, giving birth to what has been termed as internal colonialism. The domestic sector serves as a reserve economy for hard times and also subsidises the export sector through low rents and wages. It is needless to say that in the domestic as well as export oriented modern sector women with little or no skill are exploited".

Demography

According to 1991 Census of India a substantial population of 6,77,58,380 out of the total population of 84,63,02,688 of the country are tribals and thus they constitute nearly 8 per cent of the total population. There are 427 types among the tribals including the sub-tribes dwelling all over the country. The Scheduled tribes population of Orissa, which is recognised as a poor and educationally backward State along with other seven States, is 70,32,214 out of the total population of 3,16,59,736. Though the total population of this State is 3.70 per cent of the country, the scheduled tribe population is 10.38 per cent of the country. The tribes constitute 22.21 per cent of the total State population. There are 62 categories of scheduled tribes spreading over all the thirteen (undivided) districts of the State. Koraput (undivided) district is the reservoir of tribes of the State as it has 16,36,079 tribal population out of 70,32,214 total tribal population of the State which constitute 23.27 per cent. Further this tribal population is 54.31 per cent of the total population of the district which is 30,12,546 according to 1991 Census of India.

Tribal Economy

The tribal economy of India is a rural economy. As per 1981 Census, nearly 94 per cent of the tribals live in rural areas having very inadequate access to natural resource endowment. They are primitive in technology and very poor in their living. They are in possession/use of very poor quality of agricultural land which is less productive and thereby they are marginal farmers. This compels them to adopt different types of occupations at the same time for their survival such as agriculture, agricultural and non-agricultural wage labour, collection of food and other products from the forests, hunting, fishing etc. . . . Forest is all pervading so far as tribal life style is concerned as they depend upon forest for employment, food, fodder, firewood, housing materials, medicines and even recreation that is for the fulfilment of all basic needs. Thus forest is inseparable from the tribal life.

Role of Women in Tribal Economy

Women are the major contributors of tribal economy. As compared to the males the females shoulder greater responsibility of their households. In most of the cases they not only collect food, fodder, fuel and medicines from the forests but also dispose these in the nearby markets. They also work for the agricultural and non-agricultural unskilled daily wages. But the most unfortunate part of this aspect is that the females do not do same type of work throughout the year. Seasonally they engage in different activities and this can well be judged from a sample village study of Koraput district by Samal which is depicted in Table 13.1.

Impact of Deforestation on Tribal Women

Exploitation of natural resources such as minerals, petroleum and forests continues and creates havoc in the minds of the environmentalists. Depletion of forests, specifically has caused ecological imbalances resulting droughts, famines, floods, landslides etc. The forest based industries are either closed or are apprehended to be closed due to the want of raw materials. It has seriously affected the living condition and life style of forest dwellers who have totally depended on the forest for generations. The females, who are the backbone of tribal economy, perhaps are the worst victim of the process of deforestation. Fernandes and Menon from their studies in the two adjacent districts of Koraput that is Kalahandi and Ganjam have reported that the ongoing process of deforestation has resulted increase work load and low status jobs of tribal women in the following ways which also seem to be true in the case of tribal women of Koraput.

1. *Work Load in Agriculture :* Due to ban of shifting agriculture and/or because of deforestation tribal economy has changed to settled agriculture as a result of which tribal women are expected to do tedious and back breaking jobs such as paddy planting which requires long hours of bending in wet fields, carrying heavy loads and walking long distances. Further due to lack of economic and employment alternatives they are forced to become wage labourers.

2. *Extra Distance and Work Load :* Earlier when forests were close-by, women could gather food, fuel, fodder and other M.F.P. easily being assisted by children, old women and even pregnant women. But today with the forest receding to 4.80 Kms. on an average from the villages, most women have to walk for atleast one to two hours each way. This distance prevents the children, old women and pregnant women of the families to assist the working women who is to take the extra workload resulting deterioration of her status.

3. *The Firewood Crisis and Work Load :* Gupta, Desai and Ganguly (1981) have reported that the fuelwood requirements in India increased from 133 million tonnes in 1975-76 to 145 million tonnes in 1977-78 and are expected to rise to 365 million tonnes in 2000 A.D. Further it is estimated that two to three million head-loader families in the country as

TABLE 13.1 : Seasonal Distribution of Percentage Days Allocated to Various Tasks for 29 Adult Female Workers in Kangumajhiguda from July 1984 to June 1985

Period	*No. of days*	*Work on own farm*	*Wage work on other's farm*	*Other production works excluding col. 6*	*Collection of M.F.P. & food gathering*	*Total productive activities*	*Household works*	*No. work*	*Other tasks*
1	*2*	*3*	*4*	*5*	*6*	*7*	*8*	*9*	*10*
1 July to 6 July '84	6	24.7	39.0	8.1	0.5	72.3	24.1	—	3.6
7 to 26 July	20	20.5	33.1	4.1	4.3	62.0	31.3	—	6.7
27 and 28 July	2	—	—	—	—	—	—	—	100.0
29 July to 11 Aug.	14	22.4	30.3	9.1	1.8	63.6	29.2	—	7.2
12 to 14 Aug.	3	11.4	29.8	9.3	8.0	58.5	35.6	—	5.9
15 to 26 Aug.	12	16.0	33.0	9.9	1.7	60.6	33.3	—	6.1
27 Aug. to 3 Sept.	8	12.2	26.6	7.4	4.5	50.7	39.5	—	9.8
4 to 12 Sept.	9	17.6	26.6	11.9	1.2	57.3	29.5	—	13.2
13 Sept.	1	—	—	—	—	—	—	—	100.0
14 to 16 Sept.	3	22.0	20.2	7.8	1.2	51.2	25.0	—	23.8
17 and 18 Sept.	2	19.6	12.5	7.1	1.7	40.9	26.7	—	32.4
19 to 26 Sept.	8	17.4	29.9	9.8	0.4	57.5	33.4	—	9.1
27 Sept.	1	10.7	25.0	3.5	—	39.2	28.5	—	32.3
28 Sept. to 3 Oct.	6	13.0	23.8	10.8	1.2	48.8	46.4	—	4.8
4 October	1	10.7	17.8	3.6	—	32.1	50.0	—	17.9
5 October	1	10.7	28.5	14.3	—	53.5	35.7	—	10.8
6 to 11 Oct.	6	8.6	30.3	7.5	1.2	47.6	46.4	—	6.0
12 to 16 Oct.	5	13.2	35.7	8.2	—	57.1	35.7	—	7.2
17 to 21 Oct.	5	6.4	35.7	1.4	1.4	44.9	50.0	—	5.1

(*Table 13.1 Contd.*)

(TABLE 13.1 contd.)

1	*2*	*3*	*4*	*5*	*6*	*7*	*8*	*9*	*10*
22 Oct. to 6 Nov.	16	14.7	33.4	6.8	0.4	55.3	44.3	—	0.4
7 to 9 Nov.	3	—	—	—	—	—	—	—	100.0
10 to 15 Nov.	6	14.2	19.0	15.0	1.7	49.9	50.1	—	—
16 to 22 Nov.	7	25.5	23.9	9.8	0.5	59.7	36.7	—	3.6
23 Nov. to 9 Dec.	17	18.9	24.3	7.9	2.3	53.4	41.7	—	4.9
10 to 17 Dec.	8	20.9	14.2	6.4	3.5	45.0	34.0	—	1.0
18 to 22 Dec.	5	12.8	7.8	7.9	2.8	31.3	56.4	—	12.3
23 and 24 Dec.	2	12.5	23.2	8.0	3.5	47.5	45.5	—	7.0
25 and 26 Dec.	2	7.1	14.2	5.4	3.5	30.2	55.3	—	14.5
27 Dec. to 10 Jan. '85	15	16.2	17.3	7.1	5.6	46.2	42.1	—	11.7
11 and 12 Jan.	2	—	—	—	—	—	—	—	100.0
13 to 18 Jan.	6	8.3	12.5	7.7	7.4	35.9	39.7	—	14.4
19 to 27 Jan.	9	7.7	20.6	10.8	1.9	41.0	45.8	—	13.2
28 Jan. to 16 Feb.	20	12.1	12.6	6.2	4.6	35.5	49.6	—	14.9
17 Feb.	1	—	—	—	—	—	—	—	100.0
18 Feb. to 4 March	15	11.4	14.7	8.6	3.3	38.0	54.5	—	7.5
5 to 26 March	22	9.7	12.1	12.5	4.0	38.3	54.5	—	7.2
27 March	1	—	—	—	—	—	—	—	100.0
28 Mar. to 23 Apr.	27	13.2	24.3	8.1	4.8	50.4	48.5	—	1.1
24 Apr. to 17 May	24	8.4	5.1	6.9	42.7	63.1	36.9	—	—
18 to 27 May	10	7.6	4.2	0.1	49.6	61.5	38.0	—	0.5
28 to 31 May	4	10.5	7.6	4.0	43.2	65.3	31.7	—	3.0
1 to 6 June	6	6.4	7.0	0.7	37.8	51.9	44.2	—	3.9
7 to 14 June	8	13.4	31.7	2.9	6.5	54.4	45.4	—	0.1
15 June	1	0	—	—	—	—	—	—	100.0
16 to 30 June	15	15.6	30.0	3.1	2.1	50.0	46.7	—	2.5

Source : Samal, J.B. (1992) "Some Aspects of Tribal Economy: A Case Study of Koraput District." Unpublished Ph.D. Thesis, Gokhale Institute of Politics and Economics, Pune, p. 374.

a whole depend on the sale of firewood for survival. The tribal women have been traditionally suppliers of firewood. They have to cover not only long distances to collect the fuel but also long distance to sale those out in the markets.

4. *Male Migration and Work Load* : Migration of males both seasonal and long term, though not in large numbers, has many negative impacts on women. In most cases women have to take upon themselves all agricultural work of their own and have to take other outside work like wage labour in order to supplement their meagre income besides all the household work. They are also subject to exploitative elements such as money-lenders, landlords, and businessmen leading to land alienation, cheating in weighing and pricing and even sexual exploitation. After the return of males, adjustment problems arise due to change of attitude of males.

5. *Deterioration of Nutritional Status* : Deterioration and reduction in food supply has significant deteriorating effect on the nutritional status of the tribals in general and of tribal women in particular. The lower classes can afford only *mandia* or rice but not vegetables and pulses. Sometimes they starve for not getting anything to take in the morning if nothing is left over from the previous night. In brief there is a decline in the quality and quantity of food consumed by the females since they are the providers of food to the family

6. *Physical Deterioration and Ill-Health* : Inadequate and low nutrition food intake combined with the extra workload has affected the physical health of the tribals in general and of tribal women in particular. Deforestation has deprived them of their traditional medicines such as herbs or roots, derivatives of animals etc. and they do not have access to the modern medical system due to distance, lack of time and money and as a result suffer the diseases.

Suggestions for the Development of Tribal Economy through the Improvement of the Status of Tribal Women

The foregoing discussions highlights the fact that the forest based economy of tribals is in the process of deterioration and it has its serious implications on the forest dweller women. Their work load has increased, food supply has decreased, health condition has deteriorated, social status has been lowered, and socio-cultural structure has changed due to the entry of external values which is marked by lack of cohesion, frequent conflicts, cut throat competitions among the members of the community. In order to bring the tribal specifically the tribal women to the national main stream, to save them from exploitation, to raise their health status in the society and with a view not to spoil their economy, culture and social system completely, plans must be made and executed very sincerely and carefully. The following are some suggestions in this connection.

1. Regeneration of forests,
2. Community plantations,
3. Protection of existing forest,
4. Development of sericulture,
5. Development and use of fuel saving devices,
6. Implementation of health schemes,
7. Implementation of poverty alleviation programmes,
8. Encouragement for livestock farming such as goats, sheep, pigs and poultry,
9. Formation of cooperatives: This includes :
   (a) self-employment production cooperatives such as animal husbandry and dairying.
   (b) production cooperatives based on minor forest produces of local forest resources such as mango processing, honey pasturisation, gum preparation, preparation of hill and wild brooms, leaf plates etc.
   (c) labour cooperatives.
10. Encouragement of cottage industries such as mat-weaving, basket making, rope making, toy making etc., and
11. Encouragement and establishment of manufacturing small scale industries such as match box, washing soap, gums, bidi, ply-wood, seed oil etc.

Though the above suggested programmes are not new, effective implementation is yet not possible due to the following problems :

(a) Lack of awareness of tribal people in general and tribal women in particular,
(b) Lack of involvement of such people,
(c) Lack of effective government and voluntary institutions,
(d) Use of old and outdated methods,
(e) Shortage of adequate trained craftsmen and technicians,
(f) Lack of market facilities,

(g) Inadequate transport and communication facilities,
(h) Lack of entrepreneurs, and above all,
(i) Lack of adequate finance.

All these go to point out that in the peculiar tribal economy women are the real work-force and the backbone and their over dependence on forests is to be minimised, their economic structure is to be changed. We have no dearth of ideas. What we really need are the motivated and committed personnel to carry out the programmes in true spirit. Education of the tribals in this process is a pre-requisite. Not only the children but also the adults must be given education through non-formal ways which will make them free from ignorance and create realistic aspiration in them. The citizens of any developed nation are efficient, of good character, have the quality of discriminating good from bad and appreciating better ones and are in possession of high sense of duty and responsibility and this can be achieved only through education.

REFERENCES

Fernandes, Walter and Menon, G., 'Tribal Women & Forest Economy' Indian Social Institute, Tribes of India series, 1987.

Gupta, V.K., Desai, M.V.K. and Ganguly, A.K., 'Fuel, Forest and Desert' *Science and Culture*, 47, No. 11, November 1981, pp. 379-89.

Jayalakshmi, L., "Cooperatives for Rural Women", Khadi Gramodyog *The Journal of Rural Economy*, Vol. XXV, 1979.

Mishra, S., "Potentials for Forest Based Industries in Kalahandi District". Khadi Gramodyog, *The Journal of Rural Economy*, Vol. XXIX, 1983.

Raza, M. and Premi, K.K., "Indicators of Equity in Education", NIEPA, 1987, Vol. I.

Reddy, U.B., Small Scale and Cottage Industries in Project Area of Koraput, *Khadi Gramodyog*, Vol. XXXI, 1985.

Samal, Jagabandhu, "Some Aspects of Tribal Economy: A Case Study of Koraput District". Unpublished Ph.D. Thesis, Gokhale Institute of Politics and Economics, Pune, 1992

14

A NOTE ON APPROACH TO TRIBAL AREA DEVELOPMENT

— *Nilakantha Rath*

1. The tribal population of Orissa, which according to the 1981 Census constituted thirteen per cent of the population, is overwhelmingly rural in character, hardly three per cent were in urban areas. They are located mainly in the upland areas of the State which constitute the bulk of the geographical area. The villages in which the tribals are the majority, can be broadly divided into three groups:

(a) Villages which have extensive flat agricultural lands for cultivation. There may or may not be forests in the vicinity. Where there are forests, these are used for two purposes; one, for collection of minor forest products and possibly for stealing timber and bamboo, and, two, for unauthorised incursion into forest land for converting it to cultivated land. There is no shifting cultivation in these villages. These villages are mostly medium to large in size with population of more than two hundred according to the 1981 Census.

(b) Villages located in hilly areas where the bulk of the regularly cultivated lands is on hill tops, the rest terraced or unterraced on hill slopes, and low lands at the foot of hills. There is little forest land around the villages. Most of the hill top land was once upon a time covered by forest where the tribals practiced shifting cultivation in long intervals of ten to fifteen years. Thanks to growing population, the shift cycles gradually reduced to one year, i.e., it became annual cropping area. The soil on these is rather thin with poor productivity. Because of absence of significant forest area in the vicinity, the dependence of the population on collection of food, minor forest produce, or stealing timber and bamboo from the forest is very small. These villages are more often medium or large in size.

(c) Villages located in the hilly forested regions. Here the surrounding hills are covered with vegetation, fair or poor. But there is very little flat land that can be put into regular cultivation. The villagers, therefore, depend on shifting cultivation in the surrounding forest land. In addition, they collect food and minor forest produce from the forest and also steal bamboo and timber to sell. Quite often the earnings from the forest, particularly from the sale of stolen bamboo/timber, form the major source of their annual income. These villages are overwhelmingly small—with less than two hundred persons each, as per the 1981 Census.

2. Naturally, the approach to the development of the tribals in these three different types of villages will have to be different. The first type of village is indistinguishable from other similarly placed non-tribal villages, except that here the bulk of the population is tribal. The problems are the same—lack of agricultural development, of social infrastructures, etc. The approach to the development of these villages will be the same as that similar non-tribal villages. I, therefore, do not propose to discuss the approach to the development of the first type of tribal villages in this note.

3. The second and third type of villages, however, require a different type of approach. Let me begin with the third type first. The distinguishing feature of this type of village is the absence of significant areas of land fit for agriculture. It is not a question of possession of such land by the villagers. The topography of the area in which these villages are located is such that there is just not much flat enough land available to be converted into cultivable land. In such a situation, there are only two alternatives open: to shift these villagers to other areas to enable them to practice settled agriculture, or into non-agricultural pursuits; or, to enable them to develop non-agricultural type of land use activities in their village. The first type of effort, pursued by the State government in the fifties, failed. And, the fact of the matter is that the State government does not have at its disposal large areas of suitable agricultural land to resettle such large numbers of tribals. Nor is their induction into non-farm occupations away from their villages a very significant possibility in the foreseeable future. Therefore, the second alternative is the only reasonable possibility. Fortunately, there is enough physical resource

available in the neighbourhood of these villages for the purpose. And, the successful pursuit of this will benefit not only the tribal families but also the State economy as a whole. I examine this proposition below.

4. The villagers in this third type of villages derive the bulk of their poor family income from the forest area in and around their villages. This is partly from shifting cultivation on the forest land, partly from collecting edible fruits, leaves and roots from the forest, and partly from the minor forest product collected and the bamboo and timber unauthorisedly cut and sold. Investigations show that while the tribals spend a very large part of their time on shifting cultivation, they earn a disproportionately small part of their total income from it. The return to labour in this activity is very low, for the simple reason that these lands have very poor productivity. Presumably, it was better long ago when the interval between two croppings was at least ten to fifteen years. The collection of food from the forest, which occupies a part of the time of the women and children, consists of digging of edible and not-so-edible roots, collection of raw mangoes and tamarinds in season, and plain leaves, not so edible, particularly in difficult times. But all these activities do not account for as large a part of the total value of receipts from the forest as the sale of stolen bamboo and timber, which occupies as much smaller part of their time. The reasons for the small time spent in this activity are many. The fear of being caught by the forest guard confines them in such work to rather dark nights. A person cannot carry away more than a headload at a time. The forest area from which the produce can be taken is gradually shrinking, partly because of the growing numbers in adjacent villages and partly because of the forest department becoming very strict in certain areas. Finally, since tribals depend entirely on regeneration, over-exploitation at any stage results in subsequent decline in a availability.

5. If, even under such conditions, the tribals are able to derive almost half their annual income from the stolen forest bamboo/timber, it has a lesson for us. If a reasonable area of this surrounding forest is transferred to the ownership of each tribal household in the village and over a period of three or four subsequent years the tribals are helped, with wages under the various rural employment schemes, to plant mainly quick growing bamboo and fuel wood trees on it, then from the fifth year onwards these people will not only be able to derive a very much better income from their forest but will become free from dependence on the government. Let me indulge in a bit of hypothetical arithmetic. I assume that 600 clumps of bamboo can be planted on an acre of forest

land, and from the fifth year after plantation the farmer can harvest at least six bamboos per clump a year, giving a total of 3,600 bamboos an acre a year, or 18,000 bamboos a year from five acres of forest land. If a bamboo is sold a rupee a piece (the rate is much higher today) the gross income is Rs. 18,000 a year. Even if we assume, very conservatively, that he can get only half this amount from the fifth year, it is not only an infinitely better income than his present level, but a much better yield from this forest land than it might have seen in a long time. One can do a similar exercise with acacia, su-babhul, and a variety of other types of quick growing fuel wood trees.

6. Every time there is talk of giving government land, with the revenue or forest department, to the tribals, the suggestion is horticultural development, not to mention cashew, coffee, etc. There is nothing wrong with it, except that the best is sure to become the enemy of the good. Other considerations like the gestation period and the knowledge and costs of care of such plants apart, the most important thing about horticulture is marketing. The prevailing condition in the tribal areas is such that marketing will prove to be the Achilles' heel of the horticultural programme. It can come gradually, once the tribal is in a reasonable economic position to be able to withstand its uncertainties. The tribal has for long been dealing with bamboo and fire wood; he knows how to handle and market it and, luckily, there is a roaring market for both these products in the towns and the countryside. He may plant a few fruit trees, including mango, tamarind, etc., for both eating and selling. But, to start with, the major effort has to be in the direction of bamboo and fuel wood.

7. The Government, in recent years, has haltingly been moving in the direction of transferring forest land to tribals for sylviculture. First, there is the Tree-patta scheme. The tribal is allowed to plant any tree of his choice on forest land and is also entitled to harvest and sell it, paying fifty per cent of the proceeds as rent to the State. There seems to be a basic reluctance to pass on any part of the forest land on usufructuary lease to the tribal, for fear he may destroy the forest. The fear is completely misplaced for the simple reason that there is precious little 'forest; on the land the department is to transfer to the tribal despite it having been under the care, supervision and guard of the forest department. Once the tribal is convinced that the land is his for forest culture, there is no reason to fear that he will put it to agriculture, when he sees that he gets much less from such land by growing a crop than from bamboos and trees. The second thing is the fifty per cent rental

charged by the government for leasing out forest land to tribals for growing trees. This is extraordinary, when for the last half century all governments in this country have legislated against such 'rack renting' in the field of agriculture. Moreover, the agricultural land is as much government land as the land under forest. But, while the governments have charged no more than a rupee or two an acre as land revenue, and written even that little off to small owners, it is amazing that they cannot think of anything less than fifty per cent as the charge for forest land to the tribals! It is necessary to remember that the forests, not more than a century or so ago, belonged to the tribals who were evicted by the then governments in order to appropriate the forests as the first public enterprise in India. The State government, instead of rack renting the tribals, should charge a nominal rent, like the land revenue, and should, for some time to come, use the forest guard as an extension agency for teaching the tribals the technicalities of afforestation with different species.

8. In the second type of villages, there is little forest cover left on the technically 'forest' lands which are now under annual cropping. The return from such lands are, however, quite low. The soil cover is thin, and the lands, being high lands, are not easily amenable to irrigation in this highly undulating terrain. In any event. Sylviculture, to start with is the best economic alternative use of this land, though in course of time a large part of it may come under horticulture and such other uses. The arithmetic stated in regard to the third type of villages is also relevant here. The rest of the land in these villages, on the slopes and at the foot of the hills can benefit from terracing and irrigation as agricultural land. One may wonder why the tribals, knowing well that these lands can be better put under trees than annual crops, have used these for crops. I suspect, the inability of the tribal to sell such forest products, without government permission at the time of every little sale, is the reason.

9. An important question about afforestation in these two types of villages is the cost of afforestation and the income of the tribals during the waiting period of four to five years before the first harvest of bamboo, etc., can start. The present economic condition of most tribals in these villages being what it is, it will not be enough for the State government to lease out forest lands to them for afforestation, but also to help them in afforestation both with the necessary saplings and wages for doing work on their own allotted lands. Of course, afforestation cannot and should not be completed in a single year, but spread over a period of four or five years. Instead, this will ensure a regular annual

stream of produce and income from around the fifth year. In addition, there can be no objection to the tribals planting different beans to the forest area allotted to them. The tribals in the second type of villages will continue to plant and harvest their traditional crops on that part of the hill top lands which is still not planted with trees. Nevertheless, there will not only be a short fall in the income; but what is more, the very low income position of the tribal may lead him to violate the plans in some form or the other. This can be overcome by providing these villagers with wage work in and around the village, in addition to the work of afforestation. It is not necessary to mention that there is great scope for public works in tribal areas, like village and approach roads, soil conservation works, development of drinking water sources, building primary schools and primary health centres, etc. that can keep tribal wage labour engaged for a long time to come.

10. The money for the above purpose should be available from the employment oriented activities financed by the central and the State Government. Besides the JRY and the special budgets for tribal area development there are routine budgetary provisions for roads, soil conservation works, drinking water supply, buildings for schools and primary health centres. All this involves largely labour intensive work. These can and should be so programmed as to ensure fairly regular wage employment to the villagers at the time they are not engaged in afforestation. I may be permitted here to draw the attention of the Planning Board to a note submitted by me nearly two years ago suggesting a method of allocation of funds under different minimum needs programmes, in which I had proposed that only such blocks should get allocations under each head as are below the state average in their present achievement in order to bring them to the level of the State average, and so on until all blocks are provided with the facilitics. If this approach is accepted, most of the tribal blocks will get priority in the allocation of funds for the different minimum nccds programme, thereby improving their financial position for generation of wage employment for tribal workers in their villages. A proper budgetary exercise along these lines is sure to show that the resource position for this purpose is not as poor as many might fear it to be.

An Example

11. I do not have the necessary data at my disposal to present in broad dimensions the implications of my proposal for the tribal areas of the

State. But, I would like to illustrate it in a brief way for one tribal block, Kashipur, now of the Rayagada district. The data and information used here are taken from the 'Note of inspection on Orissa Tribal Development Project (OTDP) made by Shri P.K. Patnaik, Development Commissioner and Additional Chief Secretary, Orissa at Kashipur on 2-3 March 1993'. The total geographical area of the block is 1,50,590 ha. This is broadly distributed as follows:

1.	Total Geographical area (ha)	1,50,590
2.	Forest area, Gochar, etc. (ha)	32,000
3.	Unsurveyed Dongar land (ha)	75,000
4.	Uncultivable tenanted land (ha)	9,000
5.	Cultivated tenanted land (ha)	33,000
5a.	High land (ha)	28,050
5b.	Medium land (ha)	3,300
5c.	Low land (ha)	1,650

The total population of the block is over one lakh, in 21,647 households. These households are distributed as follows:

		Total no. of Households	Estimated tenanted area (ha.)	Average area per household
1.	Total households	21,647	33,00	
2.	Landless households	8,659	Nil	Nil
3.	Marginal farmers (less than 0.4 ha)	2,814	563	0.2 ha
4.	Small farmers (0.4 to 2.0 ha)	8,659	10,391	1.2 ha
5.	Large farmers (more than 2.0 ha)	1,515	22,046	14.55 ha

12. The data above show that half the geographical area of the block is what is called unsurveyed dongar land. Some estimated twenty thousand hectares out of this are put to *Podu* cultivation every year. The result is what Mr. Patnaik describes as 'a vast expanse of wasteland, which once had a dense forest cover.' More than twentyeight thousand acres of the cultivated tenanted land is characterised as high land which,

I guess, is not very different from the dongar land in its character and productivity. Two-thirds of the total cultivated tenanted land is in the hands of some 1500 households whose average size of land holding comes to more than 14 hectares, while the 53 per cent small and marginal farmers have less than two hectares each,—an extraordinary inequality, if the figures are correct.

13. Leaving aside for the movement the 32 thousand hectares of forest and gochar land, the seventy-five thousand hectares of dongar land are twice as much as is required to provide every landless household with two hectares (i.e., five acres) and every small and marginal farm household with enough to bring his individual land holding to two hectares size. All this dongar land as well as a very large part of the cultivated tenanted high land can be put under sylviculture, a use to which it was formerly put, as Mr. Patnaik notes. Since one does not know the present state of the forest cover on the land classified as forest land, let us leave it from calculation. In case of this block, it is quite clear that there is enough land in the block suitable to be given, in lots of not only two hectares each but even twice as much, on usufructuary lease to all the rural tribal and the non-tribal households, for forestry.

14. At present there is an INFAD (Intenational Fund for Agricultural Development) aided Rs. 32 crore Orissa Tribal Development Project (OTDP) operating in the block. The activities undertaken are; natural and human resource development, rural infrastructure, survey and settlement, and research and trials. Under natural resource development, there is provision for horticulture development and soil conservation which includes agro-forestry and cashew and sisal plantations. Mr. Patnaik notes that the agro-forestry plantations, developed on public lands with the help of local wage labour, 'are proposed to be handed over to the Village Committee in the fourth year'. A little later he reports the local officials bemoaning that 'the beneficiaries are mainly interested in demanding wages but the output has been very poor, there is no sense of belonging and the motivation is practically non-existent'. I would like to submit that under the stipulations of the project, it would be unreasonable to expect any thing better. The tribal villagers have not seen a forest under the management of a village committee to know what benefits will flow from it to them. The work of afforestation is also not being executed by the village Panchayat with the co-operation of the villagers. It is being executed by government officers. Under the circumstances, is it any wonder that the villagers are interested only in their wages? If the areas had been clearly marked out and initially

allotted to the villagers individually, and then the village Panchayat had been entrusted with the organisation of the work of digging pits and planting trees on all lands, under the informed advice of the State officers, it would have been reasonable to expect proper motivation and sense of belonging.

15. The difference in the result between handing over public land to the village people for social forestry and the social forestry work undertaken by the department can be seen in the Kerandimal tribal villages near Berhampur. Where the land was handed over to the villagers, they have, within seven years, created a veritable jungle on completely denuded, rocky hill slopes, by digging holes and carrying soil from elsewhere to plant the saplings and make them survive. Today, besides the wages paid to the villagers for harvesting annually the timber, bamboo, etc., from the forest, the village Kotha (common fund) receives a surplus of twentyfive to thirty thousand rupees a year that helps the 'Kotha' to routinely provide loans to villagers in need. As against this, there is the social forest in another village, executed by the government department, with sparse cover and no such consequences. Whereas, as in the successful Kerandimal village, most households have some paddy land, however small, a city is within reach and the available public land for afforestation is comparatively small, common village forest is understandable. But whereas in Kashipur, available public land for afforestation is plentiful and landlessness and poverty are abysmal, the proper thing to do is to create private lease holds for sylviculture.

16. I may end this note by drawing attention to another aspect of the OTDP in Kashipur, Mr. Patnaik's note does not give the budgetary provisions under different heads of the overall Rs.32 crore project. But, he mentions that at the end of six years of execution of the project (the penultimate year of the seven-year period of the designed core activities), 'little work has been done in the area of agro-forestry, plantation and horticulture'. Development of roads and communications and buildings for quarters and offices have taken the lion's share of interest and expenditure. One fears, at the end of this project, the approach to tribal area development though forest plantation, land and road development will be condemned, without a chance being given to it to succeed. Mr. Patnaik's note shows that the cost per hectare of afforestation varied between Rs. 3,400 and 4,400 a hectare. While I have no knowledge of the local rates and work requirements, I would think that if the work were to be entrusted to the villagers, after allotting the land for forestry to each household, the cost per hectare would come to less than

Rs. 3,000. This suggests that plantation of less than 40,000 ha would cost about Rs. 12 crores, which is well within the Rs. 32 crore budget of the OTDP. In fact, given financial resources, the tribals can be given four hectares each of dongar land for afforestation. But that is only an arithmetic exercise. The real limit is the availability of labour in the village for such work. The average number of households per village in Kashipur is 53. Assuming 50 beneficiary households per village, and 2 workers per household, there are 100 workers per village available for all types of work during the year. Their availability for afforestation work at the time suitable for the purpose and the amount of work they and their family members can do during a day, would put the limit on the extension of such work in a year. May be, the work will have to be spread over a longer period, in which case the financial commitment of the State will not only be spread out over longer period, but will become less in later years due to the tribals beginning to receive their first income from their forest from the fifth year. What is required is a clear and firm decision about allocation of land to the tribals for the purpose and association of the villagers in each village through the Panchayat in the execution of the project.

15

SOIL EROSION AND DEFORESTATION IN KORAPUT DISTRICT (UNDIVIDED)

— D.K. Pattanaik

Introduction

The environment of an organism has two components—abiotic and biotic. The abiotic component of the environment includes the Lithosphere (soil), Hydrosphere (Water) and Atmosphere (Air). The later includes all living organism both plants and animals. Various interactions between these components are too important for growth, reproduction and continuance of living being. As a matter of fact soil supports the major eco-system. The lithosphere provides the mechanical anchoragement to plants and hold water and mineral ions on which plants depend for their nutrition. It also acts as substrate for the activities of micro-organisms and animals. Soil is the shallow upper layer of the earth's crust, whose initial characteristics depend upon the parent rock material and later development depends upon the climate, topography and vegetation. The weathered rock inter-mixed with decomposed organic matter is the soil, whose formation is an extremely slow process. The top-soil is very useful from the biological point of view. It is rich in organic content, hence, of intense biological activities.[2] Soil is liable to removal from one place to another with the act of either physical or biological force. This is called as soil erosion, derived from a latin word 'ERODERE' means to gnaw out or tear away.[1] Hence, erosion refers to physically detaching soil particles from their original place and transporting to some other place. While it takes a very long time to build the soil, its erosion, in absence of good plant cover, is a rapid process. Man's involvement in some way or another is accelerating the rate of soil erosion. The accelerating frenzy of urbanisation and industrialisation by large scale clearance of forest lands leads to the loss of precious habitat . . . these are some of the malpractices that have clouded the future of the giant eco-system by offsetting the natural equilibrium. Thus resulted many catastrophes like, Acid rain, Ozone pollution, Erosion . . . etc. Again, the rate of degradation of natural resources in the rural areas is also appalling. Hence an attempt was made to find out the possible factors responsible for soil erosion and deforestation in a backward district of Orissa.

Study Area

The undivided Koraput district is situated between 20°3' and 17°50' north latitudes and 81°27' to 84°1' east longitudes extending over an area of 26,961 sq. km. physiographically the entire district has a rugged topography with hills, plateaus, pediments, valleys and perennial rivers thereby making itself a Natural Museum.[11]

General Information

A.	Geographical Area	27,369 Sq. Km.
B.	Forest Area	8,866.97 Sq. Km.
C.	Population	30,12,546 (1991) Census
D.	Literates	5,54,995 (18.42%)
E.	Density of Population	110
F.	Per Capita Land Area	0.898 ha.
G.	Per Capita Forest Area	0.295 ha.
H.	Total Roads in Km.	24,950.99
I.	Total Railway Routes in Km.	305.70
J.	Total Waste Lands	7,54.468.89ha.[14]

(All information are given with reference to[3, 5, 12]).

The cancerous degradation of forests and occurrence of extensive wastelands are the acute problems of the hilly regions in Koraput district. The district has a population of 30.13 lakhs out of which 26.75 lakhs (approximately 89%) reside in rural area (1991 Census). Out of the total population 15 per cent belong to Scheduled Castes and 54 per cent belong to Scheduled Tribes. A large percentage of this population subsists below the poverty line and depend upon the forest for their livelihood.[10] The welfare of the rural people (mostly Tribals) in general and the environment, in particular, depends substantially on the development of forest. A comparative account of the total forest area over the last four decades is furnished below.[12, 15]

Year	*Forest Area in Sq.Km.*	*Total Population*	*Per Capita Forest Area in ha.*
1961	16,196	14,98,271	0.793
1971	14,001	20,43,281	0.685
1981	12,219	24,84,095	0.495
1991	8,866.97	30,12,546	0.295

So, over a span of forty years the district has indiscriminately lost 7,329.03 Sq. Km. of forest area and causing severe soil erosion. In absence of proper plant cover erosion of top-soil is possible by wind action, floods and run-off water. Ecologically, forests influence natural phenomena like, rain, floods, landslides, and erosion. Deforestation is more tragic to the tribal economy which depend on forest for its survival. Forests are indispensable to growing demands of the local inhabitants and the industries. The predominant factors responsible for the extinction of forests are various, like, the local inhabitants who exploit the forest for their daily needs; industries which take to large scale tree felling to meet their demands of raw materials; the government which encourages tree felling for revenue requirements; agricultural and developmental causes like road construction, railways, dams, etc. and other natural calamities like floods, diseases, fire, winds, etc.[7] The enormous spread of wasteland have been created in the district due to excessive soil erosion, caused by unscientific agricultural practices, wood felling and shifting cultivation within forest lands.[14] The authors of the above paper reported that 27.98 percentage of the total geographical area of the district is waste land, which accounts about 754468.69 ha. (1991-92). Most predominant category of wasteland was upland with or without shrub which constitutes 15.39 per cent of the total geographical area and are prone to soil erosion.

Industrial Development and Its Impact

The district registers a remarkable number of large scale industries, i.e., J.K. Paper Mills, Sugar Mill, Ferro Silicon Plant in and around Rayagada; IMFA at Therubali, NALCO at Damanjodi; Sewa Paper Mill at Jeypore and HAL at Sunabeda. Not only these industries are affecting the quality of air, water and soil but also their heavy demands for fuelwood, charcoal, timber and bamboo has resulted a great damage to the natural eco-system. Deforestation and soil erosion may also be attributed to developmental projects like railways, roads and dams. Construction of roads and buildings has not only claimed forest areas, but inadequate soil conservation measures during these operations have led to soil erosion, land slides, etc.

The district also forms a part of the catchment of river Indravati, Kolab, Nagabali, Machhkund and Bansadhara over which a handful of Hydro-electricity projects have been constructed. Farvar *et al.* (1973) are in the opinion that the hydro-electricity projects have led to serious deforestation not just in the submersion areas, but in vital catchment areas as well. This in turn has enhanced the soil erosion in the catchment and siltation of the reservoir. Mohanty *et al.*, (1994)[9] presented the rough estimation of silt loss in the catchment of Kolab reservoir which has been made by the Directorate of Soil Conservation to be in the order of 17 million tonnes per year. The authors suggested an urgent attention of the catchment of Kolab reservoir due to improper management of the immediate environment.

Shifting cultivation has brought incalculable damage to the forest and is still regarded as a severe threat to the existing forest cover. It is the most primitive form of cultivation usually practised by tribals of the district. Locally it is called as *podu*. Simply by cutting and burning the standing flora on the selected land the tribals cultivate several crops. As the soil fertility declines the cultivators change the land by selecting a new area. By this practice the local inhabitants have cleared substantial areas of hill slopes, thus encouraging the tragic sequences of soil erosion. Kumar and Mishra (1994)[8] reported that about 2494 ha. of land are being engaged under shifting cultivation. Particularly the Gunupur division of the district had suffered a lot by this traditional practices. Further the practice is continued due to rehabilitation of the displaced persons mainly from submersible areas on account of emergence of many reservoir and hydro-electric projects. This is now mostly the case in the plain forests of Nowarangpur and Malkangiri divisions of the district. Migration of large number of families of Indravati Project and from Kashipur and Pottangi Tehsil had encroached the plain forests of Jhorigam and Umerkote range of Nowarangpur division.[13] Usually the tribals of Koraput have practised *podu* cultivation on the hill slopes hence accelerating the rate of soil erosion.

The execution of Dandakaranya Project for the rehabilitation of the East Pakistani refugees in Malkangiri and Nowarangpur area of the region caused the loss of many forest cover. Thousand of acres of *thick valuable forest* had been cleared during the construction of the above project. The refugees have exploited the local forest illegally to meet their requirement. Fernandes (1988) reported that 432.20 sq. km. of land were deforested for the Dandakaranya Project in Nowarangpur, Jeypore and Malkangiri Divisions. Further, the illegal felling of trees by the contractors to feed interests of various purposes is a serious factor for the current situations.

Conclusion

Hence, the causes of deforestation and soil erosion in Koraput district is a hydra-headed issue. However, the trends of depletion of the forests and top-soil is an ever increasing phenomenon where the district as well as its inhabitants suffer incredibly. Deforestation, Desertification, Pollution of Air, Water and Soil, fast depletion of Water tables and destruction of top-soil have all affected the very survival of human-being. To protect the district from the hands of disaster it is high time to create the environmental consciousness among the residents. Programmes of scientific management of land utilisation with soil conservation measures are to be developed and implemented for the local tribals under the supervision of government and non-government officials. Environmental concerns will be kept in mind while developing plans for agricultural and rural development. These programmes must meet the conditions of economic viability and ecological soundness.[4] In addition to this, suitable and systematic management procedures specific to local need are to be implemented to arrest the degradation of forests. From stone age to nuclear age, from crawling to flying; the journey of *Homo sapiens* on the road of prosperity and progress has been positive and painful. Today life is unthinkable without nature. Mankind's vary survival depends upon it. Not only all the comforts of modern life, but also the necessities are not possible without forest. Hence, conservation of the existing forest and recreation of new plant cover is a must for development.

NOTES

1. Ambasht, R.S. *Plant Ecology*, Student's Friends & Co, 10th Edn. (1990), pp. 267-275.
2. Dash, M.C. *Fundamentals of Ecology*. Tata Mc-Graw Hill Publishing Company Ltd., New Delhi, Ist Reprint (1994), pp. 170-180.
3. *District Statistical Hand Book*, Koraput, 1990-91, Directorate of Econ. & Stat. Orissa, BBSR, Government of Orissa.
4. Draft on the Meeting of the *National Development Council* held on June 1990; *Approach to Eighth Five Year Plan*, 1990-1995, Planning Commission, Government of India.

5. *Economic Survey*, 1993-94, Planning & Co-Ordination Dept., Govt. of Orissa, pp. 190, 191 and 137.
6. Farvar, M.T. and J.P. Milton (ed) 1973, *The Careless Technology;* Ecology & International Development (New York:Natural History Press), pp. 1030.
7. Fernandes, W.G. Menon and P. Viegas, *Forests, Environ. & Tribal Economy;* Pub. by Indian Social Institute, Tribes of India Series, (1988), pp. 6-10, 63-84.
8. Kumar, P. and R.C. Mishra: *Assessment of Landuse/Land cover of Koraput Dist. Orissa, Using IRS-IA LISS-I Data* (Ch. 10), Reports of Workshop on Role of NRDMS Database in Dist. Planning, Environmental Monitoring & Resource Management User's Interaction (1994), Organised by ORSAC, Dept. of Sci & Tech., Govt. of Orissa.
9. Mohanty, R.R., D. Mishra, R.C. Mishra, A.K. Mohapatro, A. Hussain, S. Das and K.S. Patnaik: *Spatial Database Generation for Kolab Reservoir Catchment for Environmental Management*, (Ch. 10). Reports of the workshop on Role of NRDMS Database in Dist. Planning, Environmental Monitoring & Resources Management User's Interaction (1994), Org., by ORSAC, Dept. of Sci. & Tech., Govt. of Orissa.
10. Mohapatro, P.C.: *Economic Dev. of Tribal India* Ashish Pub. House, 1987.
11. *Orissa District Gazetteers*, Koraput (1966), pp. 21-25.
12. *Orissa Forests, 1990* compiled & Published by Statistical Branch, Office of the Principal Conservator of Forests, Orissa.
13. Pattnaik, B.K.: *Programme of Afforestation, Land Colonisation & Horticulture Plantation as Podu prevention measures taken up in Koraput, Dist.*
14. Rout, D.K., S. Devi and S. Jena (1994): *Mapping of Wastelands in Koraput District using Remote Sensing Techniques*, Report of the Workshop on Role of NRDMS . . . user's Interaction, Org. by ORSAC, DST, Govt. of Orissa.
15. Sahoo, B. (1990), *Is It Necessary to Plant more Trees*, paper presented in the seminar *Forests & Tribal Ecosystem* on 21st March 1984 at Koraput.

16

MEDICINAL PLANTS USED BY THE TRIBALS OF KORAPUT DISTRICT, ORISSA

— *Malaya K. Mishra* and *Sudhansu S. Dash*

ABSTRACT

The paper reviews the medicinal uses of plants of Koraput district (undivided), by the tribals. Most of the ethno-medicinal information on plants collected by the scholars of Ecology and Floristics Laboratory of Botany Department of this University, which are documented, are incorporated in the paper. There are 89 plants described in this paper. Conservation for the medicinal plants of the district is suggested.

Introduction

The importance of traditional medicine which provides health service to 78-80 per cent of world population has been emphasized by Marini-Bettolo (1980). All systems of traditional Indian medicines had their roots, in one way or the other in folk medicines and household remedies, whereas some of those earliest remedies and prescriptions became widespread and were subjected to certain refinement, revisions and improvement through practices by trained medicinemen and thus got incorporated in organized system of medicine. But a major bulk of folk-medicines remained endemic to certain regions or people in the country. Due to lack of communication of intermingling and breeding of ideas and varying way of life many of these earlier remedies survived only by words of mouth from generation to generation. The lack or absence of acculturation has in many instances helped in preservation of this knowledge in almost original form (Jain 1981).

Koraput is one of the districts of Orissa rich in plant wealth. But the natural vegetation is depleting at an ever increasing rate due to anthropogenic interference. The economy of Koraput district is primarily based upon forestry and agriculture (including shifting cultivation), the bulk of commodities used domestically for everyday use are agricultural and forest products. The district with semi-evergreen to deciduous vegetation endowed with various wild plants as a natural resource. The villagers have developed an intimate knowledge on the use of wild plants in various ways. In Koraput district there are some remote villages which are independent of outside world except for salt, but all other basic requirements are fulfilled through plants and animals existing around them, both cultivated/domesticated and wild.

In the past several attempts have been made to study the medico-ethnobotanical aspects from various regions of Koraput district. *Patnaik et al.* (1986) discussed some useful plants among *Dongrias* of Kurli hills of the district Choudhury *et al.* (1975) reported some medicinal plants of Koraput district. While dealing with flora of undivided Koraput district (Das 1991), Das and Mishra (1987, 1988a, 1988b) studied the ethnobotanical aspect of the district with particular reference to Chandrapur and Deomali hills of Koraput district. Mishra *et at.* (1993) reviewed the ethno-medicobotany of *Calotropis procera* and *C. gigantia* and included all the information on the taxa collected from the district. Dash (1994) made an extensive study of medicinal plants with special reference to Narayanapatna and Bandhugaon block of the district.

In this chapter an attempt has been made to review all the available information on medico-religious and ayurvedic uses of plants, mainly based on the information collected by the scholars of the Ecology and Floristics laboratory of Botany department, Berhampur University.

Study Area and Environment

The undivided Koraput district is located on the southern most region of Orissa State, situated between 81°27' and 84°1' E longitude and 17°50' and 20°3' N latitude, with an area of 26,961 sq. km. (Statistical Outline of Orissa, 1988). The largest district of Orissa is now divided into 4 districts—Rayagada, Nawarangpur, Malkangiri and Koraput.

Tribals

Out of sixty-two Scheduled Tribes of Orissa ten tribes viz., *Kondha, Soura, Sabar, Gondia, Bonda, Koya, Paraja,* etc. are found in the district. Out of total human population 2,999,903 of the district, 55 per cent are Scheduled Tribes (1991 census). Shifting cultivation (*Podu*) and domestication of animals sustain their economy.

Climate

The wide range of climatic condition is the characteristic feature of this area. There has been a vast change in the climate due to deforestation, human settlement and shifting cultivation. Temperature varies from place to place. The average maximum monthly temperature of the district is 30.6°C and minimum temperature in winter months comes as low as 8°C and daily maximum temperature exceeds 37°C in summer, The mean relative humidity varies from 70 to 80 per cent. The mean annual rainfall for the district is 1318 mm.

Forest Cover

The official record shows that the total forest comprises about 45 per cent of the total land area in the district. Wild animals such as bear, wild dog, jackal, wolf, Indian buffalo, chital or spotted deer and sambar are common throughout the forest. Jungles of the area also favour for Leopard Cat and Royal Bengal Tiger.

The vegetation types of the district may broadly be divided into: Forest, grassland and hydrophytic vegetation.

The forest vegetation of the district is mainly of 3 categories, viz., deciduous, semi-evergreen and evergreen. The deciduous forest mainly dominated by *Bombax ceiba, Mangifera indica, Syzygium cumini, Pterocarpus marsupium,* and *Mallotus philippensis.* The semi-evergreen forests consists of *Shorea robusta, Terminalia tomentosa, Adina cordifolia, Aegle marmelos, Lannea coromandelica, Gmelina arborea* and *Madhuca indica.* The evergreen forests comprise of *Dalbergia sissoo, Grewia abutilifolia, Pavetta tomentosa, Terminalia alata,* and *Wendlandia glabrattes.*

Although the area enjoys a good deal of forest with diverse vegetation, it is under constant stress and process of reduction due to various anthropogenic interference

Plants are arranged alphabetically with the correct nomenclature, family, local name (LN) and Oriya name (Or), habit with the locality. Herbarium specimens are available in the herbarium of P.G. Department of Botany, Berhampur University (BOTB), Berhampur.

Enumeration of Plants

Abrus precatorius Linn. (FABACEAE)

LN & Or. — Kaincha.

Perennial, slender twinner, seed black or red with a black patch at hilium, Bissam Cuttack, scattered throughout shrub jungles.

Root paste is administered orally to cause abortion.

Acalypha indica Linn. (EUPHORBIACEAE)

LN & Or. — Basuni.

A perennial herb, more in winter, Narayanapatna, abundant.

Decoction of plant is used as a laxative. In case of mouth infection (particularly tongue) the whole plant is crushed to paste and applied inside the mouth cavity. The process is repeated for 2/3 times a day upto 2-3 days.

Achyranthus aspera Linn. (AMARANTHACEAE)

LN & Or. — Apamaranga.

Bushy perennial herb, a common weed of wasteland.

Sarapalli (Bandhugaon), *ca* 6 km from Chandrapur. Abundant.

(i) A piece of the root is crushed by teeth to cure toothache.

(ii) Plant juice is given internally with milk for piles and bleeding. The ash of the fruiting spike is also applied externally on piles after defecation.

Aerva lanata (Linn.) Juss. ex Schuld. (AMARANTHACEAE)

LN — Bada aluta, Or Pounsia

Suffrutescent, sub-erect herb, spikes sessile, Dumusil (Narayanapatna). A common weed on open waste lands.

The whole plant is dried and crushed to paste. The paste is applied on herpes (Or — Alati Gha). It helps to dry the affected area effectively.

Ageratum conyzoides Linn. (ASTERACEAE)

Or — Pokasungha

Erect, hipsid, branched herbs. Kumbharidhamna (Bissam Cuttack), common weeds.

Decoction of the plant taken orally to cure severe diarrhoea and dysentery.

Alangium salvifolium Lam. (ALANGIACEAE)

LN & Or. — Ankula

A woody shrub of disturbed forest. Sarapally (Bandhugaon), common on village waste lands.

Pounded leaves of the plant are tied in a fine cloth and dipped in fermented rice water for some time. To cure conjunctivities few drops of the contents are squeezeu into the opposite ear of the patient as eardrops.

Amaranthus spinosus Linn. (AMARANTHACEAE)

LN — Kantabheji, Or — Kantaleutia.

Annual herb, profusely branched in flowering stage. Dumsil (Narayanpatna), abundant in waste lands.

Root paste is applied around boils and carbuncles for easy and speedy burst.

Andrographis paniculata (N. Burm.) Wall. (ACANTHACEAE)

LN — Bhuinlimba, Or — Bhuin nima.

Annual herb, both in flowering and fruiting stage. Pannabadi (Narayanpatna), Chandrapur.

(i) Leaves are crushed with turmeric and applied on itches and other skin diseases.
(ii) Used as a powerful anthelmintic.
(iii) Roots of this species with root of *Andrographic echioides* are crushed together and applied on cattle wounds affected by larva of housefly for healing.

Angiopteris evecta Hoffm. (ANGIOPTERIDACEAE)

LN — Kakada kanda.

Perennial herb (Fern). Deomali hills, abundant.

Fresh rhizoms are pounded after washing and taken orally to cure bodyache and leg pain.

Ardisia solanacea Roxb. (MYRSINACEAE)

LN — Kutiaphala.

Under shrub. Deomali hills. Common on moist open fields.

Fruit of the plant is ground to make paste and applied on the forehead to cure headache.

Argemone maxicana Linn. (PAPAVERACEAE)

LN — Dragu gacha,, Or- Odasamari.

Erect, glaucous, prickly herb. Dumusil (Narayanapatna). Common and naturalized on the waste open fields.

Leaf juice is applied on eye corners in early morning and before bed times to cure eye inflammation and conjunctivitis.

Artocarpus heterophyllus Lam. (MORACEAE)

LN & Or — Panasha.

Large deciduous glabrous tree. Nandapur, Common among hilly tracks.

Decoction of stem bark is used as nasal drop for headache.

Asparagus racemosus Willd. (LILIACEAE)

LN — Haterikanda, Or — Satabari.

Suffruticose perennial herbs, branclets trigutrous. Dangasorada, abundant. Sarapalli (Bandhugaon).

(i) A piece of root with a piece of branch and cladocles are ground together and administered orally to ladies after the monthly menstrual cycle to check excess bleeding.

(ii) About 50 g of the root and equal amount of *'gyanasundha'* are washed and cut into small pieces. The content is gently warmed with 1.5 litres of fresh cow-milk till the whole content attains the form of butter. The content is then cooled down and divided into 15 equal quantities. To cure urinary discharges each dose is taken daily for 15 days. Non-vegetarian and sour foods along with sexual course are restricted during the treatment period.

Azadirachta indica A. Juss (MELIACEAE)

LN & Or — Neem.

A medium sized tree around village. Dangasorada, Common.

(i) Decoction of the stem bark along with leaf of *Trichosanthes anguina* (or Pitapotala), bulbous root of *Cyperus rotundus* (or Mutha) is taken orally to cure dermatitis.

(ii) Juice from stem bark is mixed with equal amount of fresh cow milk. The mixture is taken for about seven days (early morning in empty stomach) to cure diabetes.

Biophytum reinwardtii (Zucc.) Walp. (OXALIDACEAE)

Erect, reflexed hairy herbs. Koraput, Frequent along moist localities.

Decoction of leaves and roots are diluted with water and taken for insomnia.

Breynia vitis — idea (N. Burm) Fischer. (EUPHORBIACEAE)

LN & Or — Jajhangi.

A partial shade loving plant. Sarapalli (Bandhugaon). Frequent along streams and moist areas.

(i) About 20 g of root bark and black pepper (seeds of *Piper nigrum*, Or—Golmaricha) is ground with fresh cow milk and taken for eye inflammation.
(ii) Long straight internodes of the plant of about 15 cm of length is cut and the stem sap directly blown into eye to cure eye inflammation or conjunctivitis.
(iii) Leaf is ground and applied with fresh cow milk or scalp before bath to cure head drillings, for cooling the brain and enhancing the memory power.

Butea monosperma (Lam.) Taub. (FABACEAE)

LN & Or — Palasa.

Moderate sized deciduous tree, leaves trifoliate, Chandrapur at Hanumantapur, common among dry deciduous forest.

Root paste is ground with rice washed water and the paste is applied externally to cure goitre.

Calotropis gigantia (Linn.) R.Br. ex Aiton (ASCLEPIADACEAE)

LN & Or — Arakha.

Stout, hoary-tomentose shrub. Kasipur at Mandibisi, common on village wastelands.

(i) Leaf along with leaves of *Pergularia daemia, Datura* sp., and *Bambusa bambos* fomented to cure sciatica.
(ii) 2-3 drops of latex with warm water taken to cure chronic fever.
(iii) A piece of root is given to cattle with grass or straw to cure cleft on the pallet.

Canscora decussata Schult. (GENTIANACEAE)

LN & Or — Dandi Pohala.

Erect herbs, Dangasorada, occasional. Decoction of leaves used as a laxative.

Cassia fistula Linn. (CAESALPINIACEAE)

LN — Bhaluthenga, Or — Sunari.

Small tree, Dangasorada and Chandrapur, abundant.

(i) Bark is ground and applied on the forehead to cure headache.
(ii) Pounded bark is boiled with water and fomented over swelling and paining parts of the body of cattle for cure.

Celastrus Paniculatus Willd. (CELASTRACEAE)

LN & Or — Kharasana.

Unarmed, climbing shrub, Sunki ghat, frequent in deciduous forest.

(i) Decoction of bark causes abortion when taken internally.
(ii) Seed paste is used as a sexual stimulator for both the sexes.

Centella asiatica (Linn.) Urban in Mart. (APIACEAE)

LN — Brahmi, Or — Thalkudi.

Herbs, en route to Dangasorada, Abundant, shade loving plants.

Equal amount of leaf mixed with root of *Asparagus racemosus* (Or — Satabari) and with fresh turmeric are pounded to extract the juice. About 100 ml of juice is mixed with equal amount of cow butter and sugar. The mixture is then applied in the morning on head for a number of days to cure madness.

Cissampelos pareira Linn. (MENISPERMACEAE)

LN & Or — Akanabindhi.

Herbaceous perennial climber, Deomali hills. A most common herb throughout the region.

The plant (twig with leaf) is ground with about 10-15 black pepper and taken with water to cure bodyache

Cissus quadrangularis Linn. (VITACEAE)

LN — Nalaru, Or — Hadabhanga lata.

A climber with quadriangular stems. Sarapally (Bandhugaon) Common along forest.

The paste prepared out of the mixture of the plant and ragi is backed in fire. The resulting cake is taken to cure rheumatic pains on the backbone.

Cleistanthus collinus (Roxb.) Benth. & Hook.f. (EUPHORBIACEAE)

LN & Or — Karada.

Small deciduous trees, Bissamcuttack, common along mixed dry deciduous forests.

Leaf paste used as powerful arbortificent.

Clerodendrum serratum (Linn.) Moon. (VERBENACEAE)

Or — Kharakhari.

Small shrubs, 1 m high. En route Telengapadar.

(i) Decoction of root administered orally to cure indigestion.
(ii) Decoction of seed is given to reduce fever.

Costus speciosus (Koenig) Sm. (ZINGIBERACEAE)

LN & Or — Gaigobara.

Erect perennials, Arbi (Rayagada), sub-gregarious along moist shady places.

(i) Plant with rhizome (before flowering) is washed and pounded to extract juice and fresh juice is taken orally to cure filariasis.
(ii) Paste of rhizome is applied around bowels or pimples for easy evacuation and cure.
(iii) A piece of rhizome is ground and mixed with curd and taken orally to cure dysentery.

Crotalaria alata Ham. ex. D.Don. (FABACEAE)

Erect perennial herb, En route Telengapadar-Dangasorada. Common on the moist regions of deep forests.

Root paste is taken internally to cure epilepsy.

Crotalaria bialata Schrank (FABACEAE)

Solitary herbs of forest ground. Dangasorada, scattered in undisturbed regions of the forest.

Person suffering from epilepsy especially at the time of unconsciousness, fresh raw turmeric paste is applied on the scalp and forehead. On regaining consciousness a paste prepared from the root of the plant along with the faecal matter of hare is administered orally once to the patient. In acute cases three doses are prescribed.

Curculigo orchioides Gaertn. (AMARYLLIDACEAE)

LN — Totamuli

Herb with perennial erect root stock. Deomali hills. Common moist places; Dangasorada (Chandrapur).

(i) Underground parts of the plants with root of *Tephrosia purpuria* is ground and applied to cure gonorrhoea.

(ii) Tuberous root is rubbed on a stone and kept in a container. Water poured over a piece of red hot iron (mostly of the ploughing rod) is mixed with it and given to patients three times to cure enlarged spleen.

Cuscuta reflexa Roxb. (CONVOLVULACEAE)

Or — Nirmuli.

Leafless twinners,Machkund, parasitic shrubs.

(i) A twig is made into paste and taken orally to cause abortion.

(ii) Decoction of leaves given for liver disorders, jaundice and muscle and joint pains.

Datura metel Linn. (SOLANACEAE)

LN — Kaladudura.

Under shrub, en route to Hanumantapur, Rare.

Root is ground with rock salt and gently warmed then applied on the face of boils and pimples for cure.

Dendrophthoe falcata (Linn.) Etting. (LORANTHACEAE)

LN & Or — Bridhongo.

A semi-parasitic plant, En route Kasipur — K. Singpur, Common.

Decoction of bark is taken internally for menstrual troubles. It checks the excessive discharge and urine burn.

Diospyros melanoxylon Roxb. (EBENACEAE)

LN & Or — Kendu.

A small tree, 10 m high, Telengapadar, common along mixed dry deciduous forests.

(i) Decoction of bark used in diarrhoea and dyspepsia. In severity the bark paste is taken orally.

(ii) Leaves (decoction or paste diluted with water) used as diuretic, laxative, carminative and styptic.

(iii) Dried flowers to cure urinary and skin troubles when taken orally.

Eclipta prostrata Linn. (ASTERACEAE)

LN & Or — Bhrungaraja.

Diffuse, hirsute herbs. Koraput. Common herb in much variable habitat.

(i) Decoction of plant is given orally for jaundice and other liver diseases.
(ii) Plant paste used as hair oil for darkening hair.

Elephantopus scaber Linn. (ASTERACEAE)

LN & Or — Totachera.

Erect, perennial hairy herbs. Kotpad at Dongaradei, Common on the open ground.

More concentrated form of mucillaginous decoction of roots and leaves are taken orally to mitigate stomachache, dysuria and dysentery.

Euphorbia hirta Linn. (EUPHORBIACEAE)

LN — Jhotikhuntiani.

Annual herb, Deomali hills at Marichamala, Common weed.

Latex is applied on the lower eyelid, like eye black (Surma) to cure eye sore.

Erythrina suberosa Roxb. (FABACEAE)

LN & Or — Banapaladhua, Banaminjari.

Deciduous tree, 8 m high, Potangi at Sunki ghat, occasionally found on the village outskirts.

Leaf is ground with kerosene to make a paste. The paste is applied around an injury or wound externally in cattle or any other domestic animal.

Erythrina variegata Linn. (FABACEAE)

LN — Minjari.

A tree upto 6 m high, bark smooth, Narayanapatna, often planted on and around village complex.

About 25-50 ml of juice extracted from stem bark is taken orally to cure stomachache due to indigestion and for dysentery.

Evolvulus alsinoides Linn. (CONVOLVULACEAE)

Or — Bichamalia.

Perennial, diffuse herbs, Kolnora, common along dry grasslands.

Juice extracted from the plant with oil is used for promoting hair growth.

Ficus glomerata Roxb. (MORACEAE)

LN — Dumburi, Or — Dhimiraphala.

Large tree, near road sides. Papaput (Narayanpatna), sparse.

In case of pain the latex of the tree and salt are made into a paste and applied externally on the affected area. With this a plaster may also be made on the spot with the help of a leaf and left for 2-3 days till the swelling is reduced.

Glossogyne pinnatifida DC. (ASTERACEAE)

Herb, Deomali hills at Dangria hills.

Root of the plant is crushed by teeth and the content is kept over the caries (decaying teeth) for about two minutes to have permanent cure from toothache.

Gmelina arborea Roxb.(VERBENACEAE)

LN & Or — Gambari

A medium sized tree, Railaghati (Telengapadar)

Equal quantity of stem bark and plants of *Tribulus terrestris* (Or — Gokhara), Bulbous root of *Cyperus rotundus,* root of *Asparagus racemosus,* leaf of *Adhatoda zeylanica*, root of *Aerva lanata* are pounded and boiled with about 500 ml of water with a closed lid till the water content becomes half. The content is filtered after cooling. This decoction is prescribed with honey and *Piper longum* to cure rheumatic pains, excess of bile, all kinds of fever and body-ache.

Grangea maderaspatana Linn. Poir. (ASTERACEAE)

Annual pubescent herbs, radiating from common centre. Laxmipur, common on the bottom of dried pond and rice fields.

(i) Infusion of leaves taken orally to cure stomachache.
(ii) Leaf paste after diluting with cold water taken orally to cure hysteria.

Helicteres isora Linn (STERCULIACEAE)

LN — Kapelidori , Or — Mormondia phal.

An arborescent shrub, deciduous, follicles spirally twisted. Dasani *ca* 8 km from Narayanpatna. Scattered on moist shady places.

(i) Diluted fruit paste is given to women for breast pain due to excessive milk production after delivery. The fruit is also kept as such on the plait (hair).

(ii) Bark paste is considered to be a remedy for scabies.

Hemidesmus indicus (Linn.) R.Br. form. *pubescens.* (ASCLEPIADACEAE)

LN — Sana kamaraband, Or — Sugandhi.

Twinning glabrous herbs. Cymes sub-sessile, dense. Chekapadu (Bandhugaon), scattered among moist localities, Kailashkota hills.

(i) Root paste is given with fresh cow milk to infants for dysentery and diarrhoea.
(ii) Root paste is taken orally to cure rheumatism and urinary diseases.

Holarrhena pubescens (Buch-Ham.) G.Don.

Syn. *H. antidysenterica* (Roth.) DC (APOCYNACEAE)

LN — Kudhei, Or — Kurei.

A tall tree, but flowers under stress in busy form. Mandibisi (Kasipur), Palur, Dangasorada (Chandrapur); Deomali hills.

(i) Paste of stem bark alone or with mixture of other parts is given to cure dysentery.
(ii) Bark is administered to women suffering from excessive bleeding.
(iii) Bark of root and small root are ground and given for body ache.

Hyptis suaveolens (Linn.) Poit. (LABIATAE/LAMIACEAE)

LN & Or — Gandha Tulasi.

Erect, aromatic shrubs. Dharmdwar Ghat. Common along waste open fields.

Plant decoction is used as a stimulant, and causes sedative effect. About 100 ml of decoction is taken during bed time for insomnia.

Jasminum arborescens Roxb. (OLEACEAE)

LN — Saruniali, Or — Banamalli.

Climbing shrub, Deomali hills, Common on dry region of deciduous forests.

Root juice is extracted and mixed with an equal amount of garlic juice, and is given to ladies immediately after delivery as tonic.

Jatropha gossypifolia Linn. (EUPHORBIACEAE)

LN & Or — Lankakala.

Monoecious small shrubs. Bissamcuttack, scattered along fallowlands.

(i) Root paste is applied externally to cure cattle wounds.
(ii) Decoction used as a purgative and stomachic.

Kalanchoe pinnata (Lam.) Pers. (CRASSULACEAE)

LN & Or — Hemakakiri.

Glabrous, fleshy, perennial herb, Kasipur at Mandibisi, frequent on sandy ground around moist stream in lower ghats.

Leaf paste is diluted with black pepper and administered orally in dysentery.

Lannea coromondelica (Hoult.) Merill (ANACARDIACEAE)

LN — Mohi

A medium sized tree. Sarapalli. Common along deciduous forests.

Equal amount of the stem bark of the said plant and *Erythrina variegata* are pounded. A tea cup full (100-150 cc) of the extracted juice is given to cure dysentery, caused by indigestion.

Leonotis nepetaefolia (Linn.) R.Br.

LN — Tipiri, Or — Kantasidho

Annual, erect, suffrutiscent herbs, flowers red, Dumsil (Narayan-patna), Common on and around village wastelands.

(i) Flower ash is made into paste and applied to scalds and burns.
(ii) Steam-bath used to cure swellings after delivery.
(iii) Crushed root (root paste) is applied on swollen breasts.

Leucas aspera (Willd.) Spreng. (LAMIACEAE)

LN — Gagaisa. Or — Dronapuspi.

A herbaceous weed on cultivated or waste fields. Sarapalli (Bandhugaon), Deomali hills.

(i) To cure sinusitis, juice extracted from the plant is used as nasal drops into the same side of the nasal pore. Burning will continue for about 30 minutes, thereafter the patient will be relieved of pain.
(ii) About a handful of flower boiled with cow milk and the cooled content is given to patients for about fifteen days to cure anemia.

Madhuca longifolia (Koenig) Macb. (SAPOTACEAE)

LN and Or — Mahula.

A large tree, Telengapadara, *ca* 16 km from Chandrapur, Abundant.

Vegetative bud of the plant is ground together with buds of *Diospyros melanoxylon* (Or — Kendu) and taken orally to cure dysentery.

Mollugo pentaphylla Linn. (MOLLLUGINACEAE)

LN & Or — Pitasaga.

A small diffused plant. Dumusil (Narayanapatna), very common as weed.

The whole plant is dried and crushed to make a paste. The paste is applied on wounds, scabies or different skin diseases.

Momordica charantia L. (CUCURBITACEAE)

LN — Tusi kalara, Kalara.

Perennial slender, dioecious climber, Chandrapur at Dangasorada, Common on forest edges and around village waste fields.

About 25 ml of leaf juice mixed with honey is taken orally in the morning about two to 3 days to cure madness.

Murraya koenigii Spreng. (RUTACEAE)

LN — Merrsinga, Or — Bhursunga.

Shruk, cultivated. Pottangi, Deomali hills.

A beg of tender twigs is believed to cure fever.

Naringi crenulata (Roxb.) Nicols. (RUTACEAE)

LN — Ranabeda, Or — Benta.

Shrub: under stress, Telengapadar, *ca* 16 km from Chandrapur, Sunki Ghats, Scattered, under constant cutting.

A piece of the root with the root of Nux-vomica is chewed and the juice is orally taken to cure stomachache.

Neptunia oleracea Lour. (MIMOSACEAE)

Syn: *N. prostrata* (Lam,) Baill.

Annual prostrate herb. Stem white spongy as floater. Jeypore.

The stem juice is used as ear-drop to cure ear-ache. Roots used in the last stages of syphilis.

Oldenlandia herbacea (Linn.) Roxb. (OLACACEAE)

Erect, annual herb, Kasipur at Mandibisi. Common on waste open fields.

Decoction of the plant used for rheumatism and elephantasis.

Oxalis corniculata Linn. (OXALIDACEAE)

LN & Or — Ambiliti.

Perennial oppressed hairy herbs, Kailashkota hill, Common along moist shady areas, Deomali hills.

(i) Fresh juice of the plant is taken orally for piles. The paste is also applied externally on piles after detection.

(ii) Leaf paste applied over forehead to cure headache.

(iii) Plant is ground with seeds of *Cleome viscosa* and the content is warmed up and then applied over affected part to cure skin diseases.

Pergularia daemia (Forsk.) Chior (ASCLEPIADACEAE)

Syn. *Daemia extensa* (N. Jacq.) R.Br.

LN & Or — Uturuli.

Twinner on hedges. Deomali hills at Marichamala.

(i) Seven healthy leaves are crushed on palm with a little common salt and the juice is squeezed directly into the eye of cattle to cure eye diseases.

(ii) A piece of root is given with grass or straw to cattle to cure cold.

Phyla nodiflora (Linn.) Greeno (VERBENACEAE)

Wide creeping, perennial herb, Kolnora near Rayagada. Frequent on the moist open fields.

Plant paste is diluted with hot water and given for fever and decoction and also given to woman after delivery as first drink.

Phyllanthus emblica Linn. (EUPHORBIACEAE)

LN & Or — Amla.

Moderate deciduous tree, Mandibishi. Common along hilly forests.

(i) Decoction of bark is used as antiseptic to wash cattle wounds.

(ii) Fruit juice is used as an eye drop.

Phyllanthus fraternus Webster (EUPHORBIACEAE)

Sys. — *P. niruri* Hook.f., non Linn.

LN — Badiamla, Or — Bhuinamla.

Annual, erect, glabrous herb, Dumusil, pallaprit (Narayanpatna), frequent among plains.

(i) Decoction of leaves administered early morning to cure amoebic dysentery.
(ii) Fresh root decoction is taken to cure jaundice.
(iii) The whole plant crushed and made into a paste. The paste is applied on scabies, herpies and other skin diseases.

Plumbago rosea Linn. (PLUMBAGINACEAE)

LN — Lat Chita, Or — Raktachita.

Under shrub, Dangasorada, *ca* 8 km from Chandrapur, cultivated by local *Kavirajs*.

Root is ground with a little water and taken orally to cause abortion.

Plumbago zeylanica Linn. (PLUMBAGINACEAE)

LN — Sana Chitaparu, Or — Chitaparu.

A bushy perennial shrub with rambling branches. Mundiguda palaput (Narayanpatna), Common on shruby jungles.

Leaf paste used as a antidot in snakebite. Paste is applied to the wound and taken orally for immediate cure.

Psidium guajava Linn. (MYRTACEAE)

LN — Juma, Or — Pijuli.

Small tree, bark greenish brown. Deomali hills at Dhangiakokuli, Naturalized.

Leaf paste with 4-5 number of *Piper longum* seed is administered 7 times in equal quantity to cure acute dysentery.

Pterocarpus marsupium Roxb. (FABACEAE)

LN — Fuluri, Bana bija, Or — Piasala.

Large deciduous tree, leaves imparipinnate, flowers yellow. Durigenda Ghat, *ca* 7 km from Narayanpatna-Pannabadi. Scattered among moist regions of dry deciduous forest

(i) Decoction of bark administered orally on stomachache, the dose depends upon the degree of pain.
(ii) Stem bark pasted with other plant barks and taken orally twice for blood dysentery.

(iii) The root paste is used as a plaster on fractures. The roots are crushed and applied after warming on the affected area and left for 7 days. After 7 days the plaster is removed and new plaster is to be made. The process is to be continued for 3 times (i.e., 21 days). The same process is applied for cattle and other domesticated animals.

Rauvolfia serpentina Benth. ex Kurz (APOCYNACEAE)

LN — Patalagaruda.

Under shurb, Telengapadar-Dangasorada. scattered due to over exploitation, Ankadelli (Machhkund).

(i) A piece of root ground with 5-10 black pepper is diluted with water and taken orally for relief from pain after menstrual cycle.

(ii) A piece of root rubbed on a stone and then applied on the wound and also taken orally after dilution against snake bite and scorpion stings.

(iii) Root of the plant is ground and the diluted paste is taken orally to cure stomachache. A single dose per day in empty stomach for about 15 days is prescribed.

Semecarpus anacardium Linn. (ANACARDIACEAE).

LN & Or — Bana bhalia.

Tree, Dumusil, Palur (Narayanpatna) less frequent along hilly tracks of dry deciduous forests.

(i) Kernel oil is used for cough. The oil is applied on the pharyngeal wall with the help of a long stick in alternate days.

(ii) Kernel oil is also applied on cuts and wounds mixing with the soil of ant-hill for immediate recovery.

Sida cordifolia Linn. (MALVACEAE)

LN — Nelakatadi, Or — Bisiripi.

Sub-prostrate herb, flower yellow, Mundiguda (Narayanpatna), Chandrapur at Raila Ghati, frequent among bushes and tall grasses.

The whole plant is boiled first and crushed to paste. The paste is applied on fractures and swellings externally. This often tighten with the support of bamboo sticks and left for about 2-3 months in case of fractures, 15-20 days in severe swellings. With the stipulated time it cures the injury.

Solanum nigrum Linn. (SOLANACEAE)

LN — Kantabheji, Or — Nunonunia.

Erect herb, spinous, Dumsil (Narayanapatna), abundant in moist region.

Dried fruit powder is smoked through pipes to cure pharyngitis and to alleviate severe toothache.

Solanum xanthocarpum Sch. & Wendl. (SOLANACEAE)

LN — Chakdabhegi, Or — Ankaranti.

Prostrate herb, around Hanumantapur, A common weed.

Entire plant is boiled with *Adhatoda vasica* (Or — Basanga) in half litre of water. The concentrated juice is filtered and the filtrate in mixture with pepper powder is given to cure cough.

Sonchus wightianus DC. (ASTERACEAE)

Perennial rhizomatous herbs. Dharmadwar Ghat, Scattered herb along road sides.

(i) Decoction of root administered orally twice a day to cure cough, asthma.
(ii) Leaf paste is applied externally to swellings.
(iii) Latex used for conjunctivitis.

Strychnos nux-vomica Linn. (LOGANIACEAE)

LN — Kochiakhair, Or — Kara, Kochiala.

A small tree, Telengapadara, Dumusil, Palaput. Available throughout the moist region of the forests.

About six grams of raw stem bark is ground with twenty-one pepper and made into small tablets, dried and preserved. Daily one tablet is taken for seven days to cure skin diseases as well as soaring ears and complaints due to excess acidity.

Tamarindus indicus Linn. (CAESALPINIACEAE)

LN & Or - Tentuli.

Perennial large tree, Durigenda Ghat (Narayanpatna), sparse.

(i) Charcoal of bark is applied on injuries and scalds.
(ii) In case of cattle or any other domestic animal, pulp of one year old fruit is mixed with water and salt and given orally to cure fever and dysentery.

Tephrosia purpurea (Linn.) Pers. (FABACEAE)

LN — Pharaghacha, Or — Kolathia.

Bushy herb, Narayanpatna, Common on open fields in winter.

(i) The plant is crushed together with mustard seeds and given orally to teenaged girls after the monthly menstrual cycle to check abdominal pain. The dose is about 2/3 tea spoons in 6 hours duration. This also checks excess bleeding.

(ii) Plant juice is used to cure excess of acidity and rheumatism.

Tinospora cordifolia (Willd.) Hook.f. & Thoms. (MENISPERMACEAE)

LN & Or — Guluchi.

A succulent climber. Stem corky, Chandrapur, Occasionally found.

The infusion of the plant is orally administered with honey to cure vomiting.

Trachyspermum roxburghianum (Wall. ex DC.) Craib. (APIACEAE)

LN & Or — Ajamoja

Much branched erect herb, Kashipur at Mandibisi. Scattered along moist regions.

Decoction of fruit is given to cure jaundice and also other liver troubles. The same prescription is for bronchitis and asthma.

Trapa natans Linn.var. bispinosa (Roxb.) Makino (TRAPACEAE)

LN & Or — Panisingada.

An aquatic weed, Dangasorada, Sub-gregarious on large stagnant water bodies.

Decoction of leaf along with leaves of *Punica granuatum*, *Syzygium cumini*, *Coleus aromaticus*, bulbous roots of *Cyperus rotundus* and dried rhizome of ginger (LN - Sunthi) are taken in 3 doses to cure blood dysentery.

Trichodesma indicum (Linn.) R. Br. (BORAGINACEAE)

Or — Hetamundia.

Much diffuse, villous, annual herb, Kotpad at Matiadongri.

(i) The whole plant is crushed to paste and applied around boils or septic wounds. The paste remove dead foetus effectively.

(ii) Root paste or decoction is taken orally for dysentery.

(iii) Root is dried, pounded and applied to swelling of joints in case of rheumatism.

Uraria lagopodioides (Linn.) DC. (FABACEAE)

LN & Or — Khrushna parni.

Erect bushy undershrub, pods glabrous. Dangasorada at Bansadhara river bank, rare, collected once only.

To treat the infant fever, 'Haladi' (turmeric), "Daruhaladi" (yellow wood of the plant *Berberis asiatica),* "Jathi mahu," "Indrajaba" (seeds of *Holarrhena antidysenterica)* along with the above plant is boiled together and the filtrate is given in 3 doses. If the infant child is too young then the filtrate is given to the mother.

Vanda tessellata (Roxb.) Hooker. (ORCHIDACEAE)

LN & Or — Rasna.

Common epiphytes along moist deciduous forests on partially exposed condition. Rayagada at Arbi.

(i) Leaf juice used as ear drops to cure otitis and other inflammatory conditions.

(ii) Root paste is externally applied on rheumatic swellings.

Vitex negundo Linn.(VERBENACEAE)

Ln — Nirgundi, Or — Begunia.

A large shrub or an under tree, with small flowers. Mandibisi, Deomali hills, Common.

(i) About 100 ml of decoction is given to cure intermittent fever. With higher body temperature of the patient the decoction is prescribed with honey.

(ii) Leaf juice placed on caries teeth to have relief from toothache.

Withania somnifera (Linn.) Dunal in DC. (SOLANACEAE)

LN & Or — Aswagandha.

Tomentose erect shrubs, Kasipur at Mandibisi.

(i) Root used for cough, rheumatism, female disorders.

(ii) Leaf paste is applied externally on injuries, which causes swelling.

Woodfordia fructicosa Kurz (LYTHRACEAE)

LN — Dhatki, Or — Dhabatiphool.

Undershrub, Deomali hills, gregarious on open jungles.

A piece of stem is tied on the neck of a patient suffering from unconsciousness. Flower paste is used to cure dysentery.

Zingiber zerumbet Sm. (ZINGIBERACEAE)

LN — Batirikanta.

Tall perennial shrubs, rhizome not much branched. Deomali hills, sub-gregarious on the open moist localities.

(i) Rhizome is rubbed on stones with cow milk and applied on the forehead to cure headache.

(ii) Pounded rhizome is taken orally to cure rheumatism.

DISCUSSION

Pharmacognosy is undoubtedly one of the oldest branch of botanical science since the primitive man started the use of medicinal plants to overcome various ailments he suffered from. But it is a matter of great concern that during these days this aspect of information is greatly neglected. If pharmacognosy has some value, due attention is to be paid on how the plant or plant products are utilized, more particularly the method of drug preparation, its administration and the dosages should be clearly mentioned. As large section of the tribal population living in interior villages, remote forests, it cannot be over emphasized that information of all such knowledge be recorded at the earliest and scientifically tested and examined. The purpose of the present review work of ethnobotanical study is not to recommend wild plants for medicine but to draw the attention of pharmacologists for further critical studies and scientific evaluation.

Further, it is interesting that most of the primitive tribals do not accept any other medicine except the one prescribed by their herbal doctors. It has been observed that about 85 per cent of the rural population of the district depends on local traditional medicine for health care. Therefore, traditional medicine plays an important role in the health services of Koraput district. Due to its long existence, it has, in fact, became an integral part of the culture of the people. But unfortunately due to urbanization, rapid industrialization, and acculturation of the tribal environment, their culture, faith and belief are fastly changing in a downward trend. The indiscriminate exploitation and destruction of natural forests a number of taxa have already been disappeared and others are awaiting a similar fate, even before we became aware of their existence. Therefore, it is highly necessary to conserve the diverse medicinal plants of the district, which will help, directly or indirectly, to the tribal people in many ways.

REFERENCES

Choudhury, Rai H.N., D.C. Pal and C.R. Tarafder. 1975, Less known uses of some plants from the tribal areas of Orissa. *Bull. Bot. Surv. India* 17: 132-136.

Das, P.K. 1991. Flora of North-east Koraput district, Orissa. *Ph.D. thesis*, Berhampur University, Orissa.

Das, P.K. and M.K. Misra. 1987. Some medicinal plants used by the tribals of Deomali and adjacent areas of Koraput district, Orissa. *Indian J. For.* 10: 301-303.

Das, P.K. and M.K. Misra. 1988a. Some medicinal plants among Kondhas around Chandrapur (Koraput). *J. Econ. Tax. Bot.* 12: 103-109.

Das, P.K. and M.K. Misra. 1988b. Some ethnomedicinal plants of Koraput district, Orissa. *Ancient Sci. Life* 8: 60-67.

Dash, S.S. 1994. Ethnobotanical study of Narayanpatna area of Koraput district, Orissa. *M. Phil. dissertation*, Berhampur University, Orissa.

Jain, S.K. 1981, Ethnobotanical research unfolds new vistas of traditional medicine. pp. 13-36. In: *Glimpses of Indian Ethnobotany* (Ed. S.K. Jain), Oxford & IBH Publications, Calcutta.

Marini-Bettolo, G.B. 1980. Present aspects of the uses of plants in traditional medicine. *J. Ethnopharm.* 2: 5-7.

Misra, M.K., M.K. Mohanty and P.K. Das. 1993. Studies on the medico-ethnobotany of *Calotropis gigantea* and *C. procera*. *Ancient Sci. Life* 13: 40-56.

Patnaik, N., F. Bara and A. Mall. 1986. Herbal medicines of Dongrias. *Adibasi* 26: 1-4.

17

CONCLUSIONS AND RECOMMENDATIONS

Recommendations by the Seminar on Forest Policy and Tribal Development held on 15th and 16th February 1994 at Koraput (Orissa)

The above seminar unanimously makes the following recommendations to the Government of Orissa for its kind consideration:

1. There is no State or Regional Forest Policies in Orissa. Forest Policies at State level and Regional level should be enunciated keeping in view the culture specific regional practices in the State.
2. There is need of strengthening village forest protection movement and encouraging people's participation in forest protection and conservation.
3. There is need of greater commitment from political parties for forest protection and conservation.
4. There has been a constant and continuous tendency of Government to exploit forest in the State for revenue. There is need of ploughing back a greater portion of forest revenue for rural development including forest development and development of tribal people.
5. The committee emphasised that atleast one-third of the land surface of the State should be brought under effective forest cover and forest management be decided on dominant use principle by classifying our forests into : (a) Core Sector Ecological Forest, (b) Supportive social forest, and (c) Commercial productive forest.
6. Tribal people living within and in the periphery of the forest should become a part and parcel of any forest development

programme. It is necessary in order to integrate the need of forest protection land aspiration of tribal people within the scheme of forest development.

7. User forest resource base is to be created in the production forestry sector giving due emphasis to income generation among the tribal forest dwellers and the people dependent upon the forest.
8. There is need to reorient the price structure of the minor forest produce, timber and other forest produce in order to provide a fair remunerative price to the tribal people and deter forest destruction.
9. There is need for granting land rights and forest rights to the tribal gradually especially to 12 primitive tribal groups. It is agreed to start with grant of right to trees and forest produce which may facilitate land rights in course of time. Members agreed that land or forest rights should go to the tribal community than to the individual.
10. It is agreed that *podu* cultivation is a tradition and custom among the tribal people which needs to be sympathetically considered and handled by providing viable alternatives through schemes like agro-forestry schemes or national waste land development programmes etc. to them. There is need of educating and motivating the tribal people for prevention of *podu* cultivation through awareness building.
11. With reference to the orders passed by the Chief Minister relating to the settlement of tribal people in Kashipur area it is felt that there is need for survey and identification of waste land, non-forest land and degraded forest land which can be used to settle the tribal people through horticulture plantation and forest management programmes.
12. In case of major developmental projects in different sectors, the tribals and other forest dwellers displaced should get resettled on land based programmes with other assets for a sustainable living.
13. In the joint forest management programme implementation initiative be given to people in general and tribal people in particular in rural areas. The forest department and its officials should act as facilitators providing the role of determination in management of joint forests to people.
14. Tribal women cooperatives and registered tribal women groups should get support of government in getting lease of forest produce for marketing.

INDEX